FREEDOM'S NATION

A Return to Free Markets and Prosperity

JACK E. REINHARD

ISBN: 0692025200
ISBN 13: 9780692025208
Library of Congress Control Number: 2014906235
Family Publishing, Falls City, TX

ACKNOWLEDGMENTS

In my research, I came upon the thoughts of quite a few leaders who have influenced the way government finance works. Three leaders stand out. Each comes from a different time in the history of this country. The first leader is Thomas Jefferson, who played a key part in writing the Declaration of Independence that helped originate the United States of America.

Thomas Jefferson warned:

"I sincerely believe that banking institutions are more dangerous to our liberties than standing armies. Already they have raised up a money aristocracy that has set the government at defiance. The issuing power should be taken from the banks and restored to the people to whom it properly belongs."

In 1934, Congressman Louis McFadden said:

"Mr. Chairman, we have in this country one of the most corrupt institutions the world has ever known. I refer to the Federal Reserve Board and the Federal Reserve banks.... The depredations and iniquities of the Fed have cost enough money to pay the national debt several times over.... Some people think that the Federal Reserve banks are United States government institutions. They are private monopolies which prey upon the people of these United States for the benefit of themselves and their foreign customers; foreign and domestic speculators and swindlers; and rich and predatory money lenders. These twelve private credit monopolies were deceitfully and disloyally foisted upon this country by the bankers who came here from Europe and repaid us our hospitality by undermining our American institutions."

Congressman McFadden was "rewarded" for his courage with three assassination attempts, the third of which was reportedly successful.

Ron Paul, congressman for twenty-eight years and a presidential candidate, said:

"Secret negotiations established a banking cartel. It's grown ever stronger through the years. It operates independently. Rather than preventing financial crises, it precipitates new ones. We know Fed policy continues to reap profits for Wall Street while impoverishing Main Street. One hundred years is long enough. End the Fed."

Congress should be responsible enough to audit and reorganize the Federal Reserve to gain control of the finances of the United States.

TABLE OF CONTENTS

FREEDOM'S NATION

A Return to Free Markets and Prosperity

FOREWORD

This book may be the last book that I write because it is meant to have an impact on the way that our government works. My father was a high school civics teacher who revered the way the government worked for honest, responsible citizens. That was in the fifties and sixties. In 1913, the Federal Reserve was created to help the federal government fund its expenses and to strengthen the banking industry. Over the years the Federal Reserve got credit for helping the nation recover from the Great Depression of the 1930s.

A review of statistics indicates that the Federal Reserve and the government's large increases in spending failed until preparation for World War II helped revive the economy. Easy money funding by currency expansion has been given credit for recovery from many recessions since the Great Depression. In 1971, President Nixon—who was under investigation for illegal activity—dropped gold as the basic support for the dollar and currency. That decision allowed the Federal Reserve to fund federal government spending with a currency that had no physical backing with gold. Without gold backing, the Treasury could create as many dollars as needed for the government to fund government bonds with printed money. Since 1971, Congress has been able to pass whatever legislation it wants without the benefit of adequate support for its budgets. This means that if other nations will not buy US government bonds at a competitive price, the Treasury simply prints enough dollars to buy all the bonds available.

In 2007–2008, the United States experienced a second "great depression" that drove real estate values down, caused bank failures, and saw large bank losses on real estate investments. The losses were due to derivatives, or option bets, that were made on forty to sixty times the values of real estate loans. In order to support banks under its direction, the Federal Reserve dropped interest rates to near zero to ensure those banks had adequate funds to pay off the bets on their real estate loans.

The Federal Reserve has kept interest rates at near zero since that time by buying the majority of US bonds with printed dollars from the Treasury. It is now 2013, and unemployment has continued to be high in spite of positive statistics created by the Treasury and the federal government. The Federal Reserve created the boom in the "Roaring Twenties," and it also helped create the boom in the 2000s. The Fed failed to recover the nation from the Great Depression of the 1930s, and it has also failed to recover the nation in the 2010s from the latest "great depression."

The Federal Reserve's recent actions have created a national debt that will require several generations to repay. Since the creation of the first two central banks, the Fed has been criticized as an all-powerful institution that aids only large banks and the rich without considering the country's citizens. The philosophy of the Federal Reserve to always increase available funds for the federal government has created booms but has also made it slow to recover from busts. The Federal Reserve is not a part of the government, has not been audited, and must be re-organized to ensure that financial depressions do not happen again in the future.

I am writing this book to support better management of the nation's economy within the federal government. This will mean auditing the Federal Reserve, reorganizing the Federal Reserve to be part of the government, bringing the federal budget under control, and establishing a realistic value to the nation's currency. With these actions, and by reorganizing the US government to revive the individual freedom that its founders desired, the country can again be known as "Freedom's Nation."

FREEDOM'S NATION: BIRTH AND HISTORY

FROM COLONIZATION TO THE DECLARATION OF INDEPENDENCE

European colonization of the Americas began as early as the tenth century, when Norse sailors explored and settled limited areas on the shores of present-day Greenland and Canada. Extensive European colonization began in 1492, when a Spanish expedition headed by Christopher Columbus sailed west to find a new trade route to the Far East but inadvertently found the Americas. Large-scale European conquest, exploration, and colonization soon followed. North America was colonized by settlers from England, France, Spain, Sweden, The Netherlands, and Russia. By the mid-1700s, England had gained control over the eastern coast of North America, from Canada to the northern boundary of Spanish Florida.

The colonists endured many hardships in their new land. The country had little development that the colonists were familiar with from the towns and cities of Europe, and the Native Americans were often hostile. In order to overcome the unfamiliar and harsh environment of their new country, the colonists developed strong levels of independence and self-reliance.

As English control grew stronger from territories added to their American colony, conflicts increased between the local leaders in the colonies and their English governors. The American boycott of taxed British tea led to the Boston Tea Party in 1773, when shiploads of tea were destroyed. England responded by ending self-government in the Massachusetts colony and putting it under the control of the British army. In April 1775, General Gage learned that weapons were being gathered in Concord and sent British troops to seize and destroy them, resulting in militia exchanging fire with them. The conflicts became known as the battles of Lexington and Concord. The Americans were mostly fighting for their rights as subjects of the British crown.

Repeated pleas for intervention with Parliament for a compromise ended when the members of the Continental Congress were declared traitors by royal decree. As the Revolutionary War progressed over the next year, the movement for independence from Britain grew. Although the initial conflict was between the thirteen colonies and the Kingdom of Great Britain, the conflict gradually evolved into a world war involving Spain, France, and the Dutch Republic. Delegates of the Continental Congress were faced with a vote on the issue. In mid-June 1776, a five-man committee including Thomas Jefferson, John Adams, and Benjamin Franklin was tasked with drafting a formal statement of the colonies' intentions. The Congress formally adopted the Declaration of Independence, written largely by Jefferson, in Philadelphia on July 4, a date now celebrated as the birth of American independence. The formal declaration read as follows:

IN CONGRESS, July 4, 1776.
The unanimous Declaration of the thirteen United States of America,
When in the Course of human events, it becomes necessary for one people to dissolve the political bands which have connected them with another, and to assume among the powers of the earth, the separate and equal station to which the Laws of Nature and of Nature's God entitle them, a decent respect to the opinions of mankind requires that they should declare the causes which impel them to the separation.
We hold these truths to be self-evident, that all men are created equal, that they are endowed by their Creator with certain unalienable Rights. That among these are Life, Liberty and the pursuit of Happiness. That to secure these rights, Governments are instituted among Men, deriving their just powers from the consent of the governed. That whenever any Form of Government becomes destructive of these ends, it is the Right of the People to alter or to abolish it, and to institute new Government, laying its foundation on such principles

and organizing its powers in such form, as to them shall seem most likely to affect their Safety and Happiness. Prudence, indeed, will dictate that Governments long established should not be changed for light and transient causes; and accordingly all experience hath shown, that mankind are more disposed to suffer, while evils are sufferable, than to right themselves by abolishing the forms to which they are accustomed. But when a long train of abuses and usurpations, pursuing invariably the same Object evinces a design to reduce them under absolute Despotism, it is their right, it is their duty, to throw off such Government, and to provide new Guards for their future security. Such has been the patient sufferance of these Colonies; and such is now the necessity which constrains them to alter their former Systems of Government. The history of the present King of Great Britain is a history of repeated injuries and usurpations, all having in direct object the establishment of an absolute Tyranny over these States. To prove this, let Facts be submitted to a candid world.

He has refused his Assent to Laws, the most wholesome and necessary for the public good.

He has forbidden his Governors to pass Laws of immediate and pressing importance, unless suspended in their operation till his Assent should be obtained; and when so suspended, he has utterly neglected to attend to them. He has refused to pass other Laws for the accommodation of large districts of people, unless those people would relinquish the right of Representation in the Legislature, a right inestimable to them and formidable to tyrants only. He has called together legislative bodies at places unusual, uncomfortable, and distant from the depository of their public Records, for the sole purpose of fatiguing them into compliance with his measures. He has dissolved Representative Houses repeatedly, for opposing with manly firmness his invasions on the rights of the people.

He has refused for a long time, after such dissolutions, to cause others to be elected; whereby the Legislative powers, incapable of Annihilation, have returned to the People at large for their exercise; the State remaining in the meantime exposed to all the dangers of invasion from without, and convulsions within. He has endeavored to prevent the population of these States; for that purpose obstructing the Laws for Naturalization of Foreigners; refusing to pass others to encourage their migrations hither, and raising the conditions of new Appropriations of Lands. He has obstructed the Administration of Justice, by refusing his Assent to Laws for establishing Judiciary powers. He has made Judges dependent on his Will alone, for the tenure of their offices, and the amount and payment of their salaries. He has erected a multitude of New Offices, and sent hither swarms of Officers to harass our people, and eat out their substance. He has kept among us, in times of peace, Standing Armies without the Consent of our legislatures. He has affected to render the Military independent of and superior to the civil power. He has combined with others to subject us to a jurisdiction foreign to our constitution, and unacknowledged by our laws; giving his Assent to their Acts of pretended Legislation: For Quartering large bodies of armed troops among us: For protecting them, by a mock Trial, from punishment for any Murders which they should commit on the Inhabitants of these States: For cutting off our Trade with all parts of the world: For imposing Taxes on us without our Consent: For depriving us in many cases, of the benefits of Trial by Jury: For transporting us beyond Seas to be tried for pretended offences.

For abolishing the free System of English Laws in a neighboring Province, establishing therein an Arbitrary government, and enlarging its Boundaries so as to render it at once an example and fit instrument for introducing the same absolute rule into these Colonies: For taking away our Charters, abolishing our most valuable

Laws, and altering fundamentally the Forms of our Governments: For suspending our own Legislatures, and declaring themselves invested with power to legislate for us in all cases whatsoever. He has abdicated Government here, by declaring us out of his Protection and waging War against us. He has plundered our seas, ravaged our Coasts, burnt our towns, and destroyed the lives of our people. He is at this time transporting large Armies of foreign Mercenaries to complete the works of death, desolation and tyranny, already begun with circumstances of Cruelty & perfidy scarcely paralleled in the most barbarous ages, and totally unworthy the Head of a civilized nation. He has constrained our fellow Citizens taken Captive on the high Seas to bear Arms against their Country, to become the executioners of their friends and Brethren, or to fall themselves by their Hands. He has excited domestic insurrections amongst us, and has endeavored to bring on the inhabitants of our frontiers, the merciless Indian Savages, whose known rule of warfare, is an undistinguished destruction of all ages, sexes and conditions.

In every stage of these Oppressions we have petitioned for Redress in the most humble terms: Our repeated Petitions have been answered only by repeated injury. A Prince whose character is thus marked by every act which may define a Tyrant, is unfit to be the ruler of a free people.

Nor have we been wanting in attentions to our British brethren. We have warned them from time to time of attempts by their legislature to extend an unwarrantable jurisdiction over us. We have reminded them of the circumstances of our emigration and settlement here. We have appealed to their native justice and magnanimity, and we have conjured them by the ties of our common kindred to disavow these usurpations, which would inevitably interrupt our connections and correspondence. They too have been deaf to the voice of justice and of consanguinity. We must, therefore, acquiesce in the necessity, which denounces our Separation, and hold them, as we hold the rest of mankind, Enemies in War, in Peace Friends.

We, therefore, the Representatives of the united States of America, in General Congress, Assembled, appealing to the Supreme Judge of the world for the rectitude of our intentions, do, in the Name, and by Authority of the good People of these Colonies, solemnly publish and declare, That these United Colonies are, and of Right ought to be Free and Independent States; that they are Absolved from all Allegiance to the British Crown, and that all political connection between them and the State of Great Britain, is and ought to be totally dissolved; and that as Free and Independent States, they have full Power to levy War, conclude Peace, contract Alliances, establish Commerce, and to do all other Acts and Things which Independent States may of right do. And for the support of this Declaration, with a firm reliance on the protection of divine Providence, we mutually pledge to each other our Lives, our Fortunes and our sacred Honor.

The Declaration of Independence was officially adopted on July 4, 1776, by the thirteen colonies represented by the signatures of fifty-six members.

FORMATION OF THE GOVERNMENT

Before the Constitution there were the Articles of Confederation—in effect, the first constitution of the United States. Drafted in 1777 by the same Continental Congress that passed the Declaration of Independence, the Articles established a "firm league of friendship" between and among the thirteen states.

Created in the throes of the Revolutionary War, the Articles reflected the states' wariness of a strong central government. Afraid that their individual needs would be ignored by a national government with too much power, and of the abuses that often resulted from such power, the Articles purposely established a "constitution" that vested the largest share of power to the individual states. Under the Articles, each of the states retained its "sovereignty, freedom and independence." Instead of setting up executive and judicial branches of government, the articles established a committee of delegates composed of representatives from each state. These individuals comprised the Congress, a national legislature called for by the Articles. The Congress was responsible for conducting foreign affairs, declaring war or peace, maintaining an army and navy, and a variety of other lesser functions.

But the Articles denied Congress the power to collect taxes, regulate interstate commerce, and enforce laws. Eventually these shortcomings would lead to the adoption of the US Constitution. But during those years in which the thirteen states were struggling to achieve their independent status, the Articles of Confederation stood them in good stead. Adopted by Congress on November 15, 1777, the Articles became operative on March 1, 1781, when the last of the thirteen states signed on to the document.

The Articles of Confederation were used as the basis of the Constitution that was officially adopted on September 17, 1787. The Constitution provided the ability to collect taxes, regulate interstate commerce, and enforce laws. The Preamble to the Constitution stated the fundamental purposes and guiding principles that the founding fathers hoped to achieve.

The Constitution, and the Bill of Rights that followed it, gave order to the United States during its early years. After having lived under the oversight of a strong and overpowering central government from England, the founding fathers debated the power of a central government. They wrote into the Constitution and the Bill of Rights protections of the liberty of the individual and the states from an overbearing central government. The founding fathers fought for the rights of individuals and regional governments (states) to be fully represented in their central government.

A number of prominent Americans were alarmed at the omission of individual liberties in the proposed constitution. George Mason, author of the Virginia Bill of Rights, refused to sign the document, as did Elbridge Gerry of Massachusetts. Thomas Jefferson, US minister to France at the time, wrote to James Madison that he was concerned about "the omission of a bill of rights providing clearly for freedom of religion, freedom of the press, protection against standing armies, and restriction against monopolies." Aware of the lack of these provisions, George Washington urged Congress in his first inaugural address to propose amendments that offered "a reverence for the characteristic rights of freemen and a regard for public harmony." Accordingly, in 1791 Congress submitted ten amendments to the Constitution that became known as the Bill of Rights.

Amendment 1: Freedom of Religion, Press, Expression.

Congress shall make no law respecting an establishment of religion, or prohibiting the free exercise thereof; or abridging the freedom of speech, or of the press; or the right of the people peaceably to assemble, and to petition the Government for a redress of grievances.

Amendment 2: Right to Bear Arms.

A well-regulated Militia, being necessary to the security of a free State, the right of the people to keep and bear Arms, shall not be infringed.

Amendment 3: Quartering of Soldiers.

No Soldier shall, in time of peace be quartered in any house, without the consent of the Owner, nor in time of war, but in a manner to be prescribed by law.

Amendment 4: Search and Seizure.

The right of the people to be secure in their persons, houses, papers, and effects, against unreasonable searches and seizures, shall not be violated, and no Warrants shall issue, but upon probable cause, supported by Oath or affirmation, and particularly describing the place to be searched, and the persons or things to be seized.

Amendment 5: Trial and Punishment, Compensation for Takings.

No person shall be held to answer for a capital, or otherwise infamous crime, unless on a presentment or indictment of a Grand Jury, except in cases arising in the land or naval forces, or in the Militia, when in actual service in time of War or public danger; nor shall any person be subject for the same offense to be twice put in jeopardy of life or limb; nor shall be compelled in any criminal case to be a witness against himself, nor be deprived of life, liberty, or property, without due process of law; nor shall private property be taken for public use, without just compensation.

Amendment 6: Right to Speedy Trial, Confrontation of Witnesses.

In all criminal prosecutions, the accused shall enjoy the right to a speedy and public trial, by an impartial jury of the State and district wherein the crime shall have been committed, which district shall have been previously ascertained by law, and to be informed of the nature and cause of the accusation; to be confronted with the witnesses against him; to have compulsory process for obtaining witnesses in his favor, and to have the Assistance of Counsel for his defense.

Amendment 7: Trial by Jury in Civil Cases.

In Suits at common law, where the value in controversy shall exceed twenty dollars, the right of trial by jury shall be preserved, and no fact tried by a jury, shall be otherwise re-examined in any Court of the United States, than according to the rules of the common law.

Amendment 8: Cruel and Unusual Punishment.

Excessive bail shall not be required, nor excessive fines imposed, nor cruel and unusual punishments inflicted.

Amendment 9: Construction of Constitution.

The enumeration in the Constitution, of certain rights, shall not be construed to deny or disparage others retained by the people.

Amendment 10 - Powers of the States and People.

The powers not delegated to the United States by the Constitution, nor prohibited by it to the States, are reserved to the States respectively, or to the people.

The US Constitution, adopted in 1787, was in many ways a work of creative genius. It established that the entire nation stretching then from Maine to Georgia and from the Atlantic Ocean to the Mississippi Valley was a unified, or "common," market. There were no tariffs or taxes on interstate commerce. The Constitution provided that the federal government could regulate commerce with foreign nations and among the states, establish uniform bankruptcy laws, create money and regulate its value, fix standards of weights and measures, establish post offices and roads, and fix rules governing patents and copyrights.

FIRST-CENTURY BUSINESS GROWTH

Alexander Hamilton, one of the nation's founding fathers and its first secretary of the treasury, advocated an economic development strategy in which the federal government would take a strong role in nurturing infant industries. He also urged the federal government to create a national bank and to assume the public debts that the colonies had incurred during the Revolutionary War. Though the new government dallied over some of Hamilton's proposals, it ultimately did make tariffs an essential part of American foreign policy. Although early American farmers feared that a national bank would serve the rich at the expense of the poor, the first national Bank of the United States was chartered in 1791 and lasted until 1811.

Hamilton's political rival, Thomas Jefferson, based his philosophy on protecting the common man from political and economic tyranny. In 1801, Jefferson became president (1801–1809) and promoted a more decentralized, agrarian democracy. Andrew Jackson became president in 1829 and opposed the successor to Hamilton's National Bank, which he believed favored the entrenched interests of the Eastern against the Western United States. When he was elected for a second term, Jackson opposed renewing the second National Bank's charter, and Congress supported him. President Andrew Jackson vetoed legislation to renew the Second Bank of the United States, starting a period of free banking. Jackson staked his second term on the issue of central banking, stating, "Every monopoly and all exclusive privileges are granted at the expense of the public, which ought to receive a fair equivalent. The many millions which this act proposes to bestow on the stockholders of the existing bank must come directly or indirectly out of the earnings of the American people." Jefferson felt that the earnings by a central bank should be the result of services performed by the bank and not simply a transfer of profits from people to bank stockholders. Until the Civil War, the nation's finances were supported by tariffs and land sales as the country developed its territory.

The **American Civil War**, also known as the **War Between the States**, or simply the **Civil War** in the United States, was a civil war fought from 1861 to 1865 in the United States after several Southern states declared their secession and formed the Confederate States of America (the "Confederacy" or the "South"). The states that remained were known as the "Union" or the "North." The war had its origin in the fractious issue of the extension of slavery into the western territories. Foreign powers did not intervene. After four years of bloody combat that left over six hundred thousand soldiers dead and destroyed much of the South's infrastructure, the Confederacy collapsed, slavery was abolished, and the difficult Reconstruction process of restoring national unity and guaranteeing rights to the freed slaves began.

The Industrial Revolution began in Europe in the late eighteenth and early nineteenth centuries and quickly spread to the United States. Cotton, at first a small-scale crop in the South, boomed following Eli Whitney's invention in 1793 of the cotton gin, a machine that separated raw cotton from seeds and other waste. Planters in the South bought land from small farmers who frequently moved farther west. Soon, large plantations, supported by slave labor, made some families very wealthy. By 1860, when Abraham Lincoln was elected president, 16 percent of the US population lived in urban areas, and a third of the nation's income came from manufacturing. Urbanized industry was limited primarily to the Northeast; cotton cloth production was the leading industry, with the manufacture of shoes, woolen clothing, and machinery.

In 1863, as a means to help finance the Civil War, a system of national banks was instituted by the National Currency Act. The banks each had the power to issue standardized national bank notes based on US bonds held by the bank. The Act was totally revised in 1864 and later renamed as the National Bank Act, or National Banking Act, as it is popularly known. The administration of the new national banking system was vested in the newly created Office of the Comptroller of the Currency and its chief administrator, the Comptroller of the Currency. The Office, which still exists today, examines and supervises all banks chartered nationally and is a part of the US Treasury Department.

At the time of passage of the Constitution and the Bill of Rights, the United States had many individuals who were indentured servants or slaves. Though some of the signers of the Constitution and Bill of Rights owned slaves, some did not approve of slavery or owning individuals. The slavery issue was settled as a result of the Civil War or War Between the States. In 1866, the Thirteenth Amendment gave Civil Rights to all who were born or naturalized inhabitants of the United States. As a follow-up to that amendment, the Fourteenth Amendment was passed shortly afterward to give the same rights to inhabitants within each state. Both of these amendments were the result of abolishing slavery within the United States. Though slavery was removed and freedom of the individual was now granted, those amendments, coupled with the Constitution and the Bill of Rights, were in line with the intentions of the founding fathers of the nation.

After the Fourteenth Amendment was ratified and became part of the Constitution, all individual citizens could truly live up to the Declaration of Independence. The following is from the Declaration of Independence:

"We hold these truths to be self-evident, that all men are created equal, that they are endowed by their Creator with certain unalienable rights. That among these are Life, Liberty, and the pursuit of Happiness."

Now, all citizens, no matter what their backgrounds, were free to pursue their futures as they saw fit.

Although the Civil War and the Thirteenth and Fourteenth Amendments established the central government as a stronger political power over the states, it also reinforced the importance of the individual. The issue of whether central government should rule, as did Great Britain, was not established. The central government was established as a power over the states, but the power and freedom of the individual was finally set in place.

Northern victory in the US Civil War (1861–1865), however, sealed the destiny of the nation and its economic system. The rapid economic development following the Civil War laid the groundwork for the modern US industrial economy. The "Gilded Age" of the second half of the nineteenth century was the epoch of businessmen who amassed vast financial empires. Often their success lay in seeing the long-range potential of a new service or product. During this period, business interests acquired significant influence over government.

In the early years of American history, most political leaders were reluctant to involve the federal government too heavily in the private sector. In general, they accepted the concept of laissez-faire, a doctrine that opposed government interference in the economy except to maintain law and order. This attitude started to change during the latter part of the nineteenth century. Then small business, farm, and labor movements began asking the government to ensure competition and free enterprise. National bank currency was considered inelastic because it was based on the fluctuating value of US Treasury bonds rather than the growing desire for easy credit. If Treasury bond prices declined, a national bank had to reduce the amount of currency it had in circulation by either refusing to make new loans or by calling in loans it had made already.

The related liquidity problem was largely caused by an immobile, pyramidal reserve system, in which nationally chartered country banks were required to set aside their reserves in reserve city banks, which in turn were required to have reserves in central city banks. During planting season, country banks needed to call in their reserves, and during the harvest season they would add to their reserves. A national bank whose reserves were being drained would replace its reserves by selling stocks and bonds, by borrowing from a clearinghouse or by calling in loans. As there was little in the way of deposit insurance, if a bank was rumored to be having liquidity problems, then it might cause many people to remove their funds from the bank.

Because of the crescendo effect of banks that lent more than their assets could cover, during the last quarter of the nineteenth century and the beginning of the twentieth century, the US economy went through a series of financial panics. Although there were "panics" (bank failures) in 1873 and 1893 that caused reductions in industrial development, in 1890 the United States surpassed Great Britain in manufacturing output. The growth of the US economy during the nineteenth century was due to the constitutional guidelines of the free enterprise system that the founding fathers had set up, and the freedom that individuals gained from it. The trading and marketing actions that were successful by individuals and businesses under the free market contributed to the growth of industry and agriculture in the US economy. With the growth in industrial development and agricultural development, and the expanded national transportation system, the need for capital placed banking as the major industry with minimal regulation.

REGULATION GROWTH AND THE FEDERAL RESERVE

During the years between 1900 and 1920, many long-standing regulatory agencies were created. The Interstate Commerce Commission, the Federal Trade Commission, the Federal Reserve Board, and the income tax were instituted. The increased creation of regulatory agencies was a reaction by the federal government to continue providing fair and reasonable growth as had developed during the last half of the eighteenth century.

There had been banking panics (bank failures) during the nineteenth century because of massive withdrawals of funds from banks due to a loss of faith in their management. The panics were caused by the use of fractional reserve allowances for loans and poor bank judgment of loan risks. A particularly severe panic in 1907 renewed demands for banking and currency reform. The following year Congress enacted the Aldrich-Vreeland Act, which provided for an emergency currency and established the National Monetary Commission to study banking and currency reform. The banking panic of 1907 encouraged leading representatives of the major banking interests of that period to meet at J. P. Morgan's Jekyll Island Club in 1910 to set up the structure of a central bank. J.P. Morgan was the nation's largest bank, and Morgan was the central bank's founder. The plan was submitted to the National Monetary Commission in 1911, and the Federal Reserve Act was passed by Congress in 1913.

After months of hearings, amendments, and debates, the Federal Reserve Act passed Congress in December 1913. The bill passed the House by an overwhelming majority of 298 to 60 on December 22, 1913, and passed the Senate the next day by a vote of forty-three to twenty-five. An earlier version of the bill had passed the Senate fifty-four to thirty-four, but almost thirty senators had left for Christmas vacation by the time the final bill came to a vote. Most Democrats supported it, and most Republicans were against it.

While a system of twelve regional banks was designed so as not to give eastern bankers too much influence over the new bank, in practice, the Federal Reserve Bank of New York became "first among equals." The New York Fed, for example, is solely responsible for conducting open-market operations at the direction of the Federal Open Market Committee. Democratic Congressman Carter Glass sponsored and wrote the accompanying legislation, and his home state capital of Richmond, Virginia, was made a district headquarters. Democratic Senator James A. Reed of Missouri obtained two districts for his state. However, the 1914 report of the Federal Reserve Organization Committee, which clearly laid out the rationale for their decisions on establishing Reserve Bank districts in 1914, showed that it was based almost entirely upon current correspondent banking relationships.

To quell Elihu Root's objections to possible inflation, the passed bill included provisions that the bank must hold at least 40 percent of its outstanding loans in gold. (In later years, to stimulate short-term economic activity, Congress would amend the act to allow more discretion in the amount of gold that must be redeemed by the Bank.) Critics of the time (later joined by economist Milton Friedman) suggested that Glass's legislation was almost entirely based on the Aldrich Plan, which had been derided as giving too much power to elite bankers. Glass denied copying Aldrich's plan. In 1922, he told Congress, "No greater misconception was ever projected in this Senate chamber."

With regard to creation of the Federal Reserve, the Comptroller of the Currency issued a statement that assured citizens that a closer watch on banks would virtually ensure the elimination of bank failures. The operation of the Federal Reserve System was to provide flexibility for the funding of government expenditures and to adjust to variances in the country's economy. What the Federal Reserve Act did was to eliminate the laissez-faire government philosophy that had made the United States the leading economy in the world at that time.

Shortly after the creation of the Federal Reserve, the United States entered World War I. The 1917 War Revenue Act raised taxes while the government sold bonds to the general public and the newly founded Federal Reserve. At the time, America was clinging to a gold standard to back its currency, to avoid simply printing additional money and to help preserve the standard while preventing inflation. However, the war altered the American economy in many ways. Taxes were lowered after the war but remained higher than before it. The Federal Reserve assumed a more dominant role as New York became the financial center of the world.

The federal government, in short, showed that it could be a dominant force in the American economy. With lower taxes and confidence in the Federal Reserve central bank, the country's economy grew quickly. The end of the war in Europe opened those markets to US industrial and agricultural products. The economic prosperity and activity from postwar consumerism became known as the "Roaring Twenties." When the decade came to a crashing halt in 1929, the government was obligated to play a dominant role.

THE GREAT DEPRESSION OF THE 1930S

On October 29, 1929, the stock market crashed in New York. The stock market crash set off a chain of events leading to many bankruptcies of people, banks, and companies. The "Roaring Twenties" encouraged the thinking that accepted high risk supported by low credit requirements. When the risk got out of hand in the stock market and in banking, it was a shock that developed into a panic that evolved into the "Great Depression," which spread throughout the business world. Prior to the stock market crash, tax levels on income had been lowered, and margin requirements on stock purchases were only 10 percent. This meant that only ten dollars was needed to buy one hundred dollars' worth of stock. Following the "Roaring Twenties," normal variances in economic activity, with downturns or slowing of the economy, were to be expected. The potential reduction in economic activity, coupled with ridiculously high margin allowances, made the crash possible. The confidence in the financial system supported by the Federal Reserve, and the banking interests that oversaw it, made risk too easy to accept. The government, reacting to the reduced economic activity, passed the Smoot-Hawley Tariff Act (enacted June 17, 1930), which worsened the depression by seriously reducing international trade and causing retaliatory tariffs in other countries.

After the panic of 1929, and during the first ten months of 1930, 744 US banks failed. (In all, nine thousand banks failed during the 1930s.) By April 1933, around $7 billion in deposits had been frozen in failed banks or those left unlicensed after the March Bank Holiday. The words of the Comptroller of the Currency in 1913 were no longer considered true.

British economist John Maynard Keynes argued in *General Theory of Employment Interest and Money* that governments have to run deficits when the economy is slowing, as the private sector would not invest enough to keep production at the normal level and bring the economy out of recession. Keynesian economists called on governments during times of economic crisis to pick up the slack by increasing government spending or cutting taxes or both. As the Depression wore on, Franklin D. Roosevelt tried public works, farm subsidies, and other devices to restart the US economy, but he never completely gave up trying to balance the budget. According to the Keynesians, this improved the economy, but Roosevelt never spent enough to bring the economy out of recession until the start of World War II.

Keynes's philosophy did not work in the Great Depression. The philosophy means that the next generation has to pay for deficit spending because of transfer of costs to the public by inflation or taxes. The term "kicking the can down the road" is used by today's politicians as an excuse for wasting taxpayers' money today with bills coming due through taxes or inflation. The Keynesian philosophy is followed by most current members of the Federal Reserve Board and its chairman, in addition to many members of the current Congress.

A competing philosophy to that of Keynes is the Austrian theory. The Austrian philosophy can be described as that of the free market and rational asset investing by the individual. This method of thinking conflicts with the central government or statist belief that all individuals require direction to reach the same conclusion. A government-controlled market varies most often from one that follows the rational free-market guideline of supply and demand when applied to each individual. During times of crisis, such as the Depression of the 1930s, central government actions will rarely be able to benefit a country as a whole. It is only normal for individuals to desire what best fits their objectives for themselves and their families. Individuals, as God made them, do not desire to follow the direction of others, and particularly the direction of a singular entity such as a government. Consequently, in a time of crisis such as the Great Depression, the combined effort of individuals will not provide results that fit each person's objectives.

Working for the government was unsuccessful in the 1930s because work that was generated by growth in the private market had fallen. Government-sponsored work, though it provided income, did not satisfy the basic need for individual accomplishment and growth in the economy. God gave each individual the ability to make his or her own choices, so that each could reach the level of the Supreme Being in the afterlife. The founders of this country were Christians who understood this thinking and provided the ability for each individual to attain his or her own maximum capability through the guidance of the Constitution.

The extent to which the spending for relief and public works provided a sufficient stimulus to revive the depressed US economy—or whether it harmed the economy—can be debated. If one defines economic health entirely by the gross domestic product, the United States had gotten back on track by 1934 and made a full recovery by 1936; but as Roosevelt said, one third of the nation was ill-fed, ill-housed and ill-clothed. The GNP was 34 percent higher in 1936 than in 1932, and 58 percent higher in 1940, on the eve of war. The economy grew 58 percent from 1932 to 1940 during eight years of peacetime, and then grew another 56 percent from 1940 to 1945 during five years of war. The unemployment rate fell from 25.2 percent in 1932 to 13.9 percent in 1940, when the draft started. New Deal reforms included Social Security, the Securities and Exchange Commission, the Federal Deposit Insurance Corporation, and Fannie Mae. No doubt preparation for war was the main reason for increased economic activity, in spite of stronger activity by the federal government.

It took a World War to focus the nation on fighting for the single cause of avoiding two countries whose militaries were attempting to take away the country's freedom. The country was motivated by the threat of the loss of the freedom for which the United States had been created. During the war, the economy operated under so many different conditions that comparing it with the peacetime economy is impossible. During wartime, massive spending, price controls, bond campaigns, controls over raw materials, prohibitions on new housing and new automobiles, rationing, guaranteed cost-plus profits, subsidized wages, and the draft of twelve million soldiers were not normal activities.

During the 1941–1945 war years, the War Production Board coordinated the nation's productive capabilities so that military priorities would be met. Converted consumer-products plants filled many military orders. Automakers built tanks and aircraft, causing the United States to become known as the "arsenal of democracy." To avoid inflation, the newly created Office of Price Administration controlled rents on some dwellings, rationed consumer items ranging from sugar to gasoline, and otherwise tried to restrain price increases. Six million women took newly created temporary jobs in munitions, manufacturing, and production. Some women were replacing men who were away in the military. These working women were symbolized by the fictional character of Rosie the Riveter. After the war, many women returned to household work as men returned from military service. The nation turned to the suburbs, as a pent-up demand for new housing was finally unleashed.

THE GROWING STRENGTH OF THE FEDERAL RESERVE AND THE 1951 ACCORD

After the war years, between 1947 and 1951, conflicts arose between the Treasury and the Fed on monetary policy that could address changes in unemployment and inflation. The country experienced a recession in 1948 and 1949. In 1950, with the recession over, inflation and the need for monetary restraint once more became policy concerns. During January and February 1951, the Treasury attempted to bind the Fed to the maintenance of low interest rates through public announcements. The Secretary of the Treasury, John Snyder, announced that consultations with President Truman and the chairman of the Federal Reserve Board had led to a decision that new long-term debt issues would continue to be offered at a 2.5 percent interest rate—a view apparently not shared by the Fed.

When the Fed's disagreement became known, President Truman called the entire FOMC to a White House meeting to discuss policy. The White House and the Treasury then announced that the Fed would continue to support government bond prices. Marriner Eccles, who was still a member of the Board of Governors, released the Fed's confidential minutes of the White House meeting—minutes that contradicted the White House and Treasury claims of a Fed commitment to keep rates fixed. As a result of these public disputes, the Fed asked the president to initiate negotiations between the Treasury and the Federal Reserve. While the president established a formal committee to resolve the issues of conflict, the actual "accord" between the two institutions was worked out directly between Federal Reserve and Treasury officials. On March 4, 1951, the accord was announced to the public: "The Treasury and the Federal Reserve System have reached full accord with respect to debt-management and monetary policies to be pursued in furthering their common purpose to assure the successful financing of the Government's requirements and, at the same time, to minimize monetization of the public debt."

The 1951 Accord did seem to give the Fed independence in conducting monetary policy. However, the president can nominate the chairman of the Federal Reserve Board, who can then be confirmed by the Senate. This of course, gives much political power to the board chairman if he or she can please the president and Congress by providing an aggressive monetary policy to aid them in gaining votes through new benefit programs. The 1951 Accord aided the growth of the United States after the war and thus helped ensure a stronger money supply to foster that growth.

The period from the end of World War II to the early 1970s was a golden era of American capitalism. Two hundred billion dollars in war bonds matured, and the GI Bill financed a well-educated work force. The middle class swelled, as did GDP and productivity. The United States underwent a terrific age of economic growth. This growth was distributed fairly evenly across the economic classes, which historians attribute to the strength of labor unions during this period. (Labor union membership peaked in the United States during the 1950s, in the midst of this massive economic growth.)

Much of the growth came from the movement of low-income farmworkers into better-paying jobs in the towns and cities—a process largely completed by 1960. Congress created the Council of Economic Advisors to promote high employment, high profits, and low inflation. The Eisenhower administration (1953–1961) supported an activist contra cyclical approach that helped to establish Keynesianism as a bipartisan economic policy for the nation. Especially important in formulating the CEA response to the recession—which accelerated public works programs, eased credit, and reduced taxes—were Arthur F. Burns and Neil H. Jacoby.

"I am now a Keynesian in economics," proclaimed Republican President Richard Nixon in 1969. Although this period brought economic expansion to the country as whole, it was not recession proof. The recessions of 1945, 1949, 1953, 1958, and 1960 saw a drastic decline in GDP. The Federal Reserve and its use of Keynesianism increased the money supply in each recession to end the recessions with increased growth of the economy. Federal taxes on incomes, profits, and payrolls had risen to high levels of 90 percent during World War II. Those rates had been cut back only slowly, with the highest income tax for individuals remaining until 1964. With high tax rates and high employment in the 1950s, the Keynesian money supply increases avoided inflation and reduced the standard of living for most consumers. Adherence to the gold standard also helped limit spending and minimized inflationary pressures during this high-growth period of the nation's economy.

The "baby boom" saw a dramatic increase in fertility during the period from 1942 to 1957. The boom was also a response to delayed marriages and childbearing during the Depression and war years. The growth of families, a surge in prosperity, a demand for suburban single-family homes (as opposed to inner-city apartments), and new optimism about the future further contributed to this high growth period. The boom crested at about 1957 and then slowly declined.

The growth in the economy continued into the 1960s, right up to when the United States became involved in Vietnam under Presidents Eisenhower and Kennedy. Initial US involvement was to contain the expansion of communism in Asia, where France had governed since the 1940s. When France withdrew from French Indochina, the United States became involved in supporting the South Vietnamese government against the North Vietnamese government. The North Vietnamese were supported by China. The US goal was to stem the growth of communism that had been stopped in Korea by US military in South Korea. It was theorized that continued US action was needed in South Vietnam to stop the spread of communism in Asia. Although the United States became involved in the early 1960s, its main involvement was between 1965 and 1975. Between 1965 and 1975, the United States spent $111 billion on the war ($686 billion in FY 2008 dollars). This resulted in a large and growing federal budget deficit.

More than three million Americans served in the Vietnam War, some 1.5 million of whom actually saw combat in Vietnam. James E. Westheider wrote that "at the height of American involvement in 1968, for example, there were 543,000 American military personnel in Vietnam, but only 80,000 were considered combat troops." Conscription in the United States had been controlled by the president since World War II, but the draft ended in 1973. By war's end, 58,220 American soldiers had been killed, more than 150,000 had been wounded, and at least 21,000 had been permanently disabled. The average age of the US troops killed in Vietnam was 23.11 years. It was estimated that of those killed in combat, 86.3 percent were white, 12.5 percent were black, and the remainder were from other races. Approximately 830,000 Vietnam veterans suffered symptoms of posttraumatic stress disorder. An estimated 125,000 Americans left for Canada to avoid the Vietnam draft, and approximately 50,000 American servicemen deserted. In 1977, President Jimmy Carter granted a full, complete, and unconditional pardon to all Vietnam-era draft dodgers. The Vietnam War POW and MIA issue, concerning the fate of US service personnel listed as missing in action, persisted for many years after the war's conclusion. As of 2013, the US government is paying Vietnam veterans and their families or survivors more than $22 billion a year in war-related claims.

The Vietnam War also took its toll on the people of Vietnam, Cambodia, and Laos. It was estimated that 195,000 to 430,000 South Vietnamese civilians and 50,000 to 65,000 North Vietnamese civilians died in the war. The Army of the Republic of Vietnam lost between 171,331 and 220,357 men during the war. The official US Department of Defense figure was 950,765 communist forces killed in Vietnam from 1965 to 1974. Defense Department officials believed that these body-count figures needed to be deflated by 30 percent. In addition, Guenter Lewy assumes that one-third of the reported "enemies" killed may have been civilians; he concludes that the actual number of deaths of communist military forces was probably closer to 444,000. The most detailed demographic study calculated 791,000 to 1,141,000 war-related deaths for all of Vietnam. Between two hundred thousand and three hundred thousand Cambodians died in the war, along with about sixty thousand Laotians. Without a doubt, the Vietnam War was costly in lives of all combatants. There is little justification for the involvement by the United States in Vietnam based on the outcome of the war and the history of the region in the years following it.

As the 1960s progressed, increasing numbers of young people began to revolt against the social norms and conservatism of the 1950s and early 1960s, as well as the escalation of the Vietnam War and Cold War. A social revolution swept through the country to create a more liberated society. As the Civil Rights Movement progressed, feminism and environmentalism movements soon grew in the midst of a Sexual Revolution, with its distinctive protest forms, from long hair to rock music.

THE CENTRAL GOVERNMENT'S RISE WITH THE GREAT SOCIETY AND WAR ON POVERTY

The assassination of Kennedy in 1963 helped change the political mood of the country. The new president, Lyndon B. Johnson, capitalized on this situation, using a combination of the national mood and his own political savvy to push Kennedy's agenda, most notably the Civil Rights Act of 1964 and the 1965 Voting Rights Act. Two main goals of the Great Society social reforms were the elimination of poverty and racial injustice. New major spending programs that addressed education, medical care, urban problems, and transportation were launched during this period. The government financed some of private industry's research and development throughout these decades, most notably ARPANET (which would become the Internet). The Great Society in scope and sweep resembled the New Deal domestic agenda of Franklin D. Roosevelt in the 1930s but differed sharply in types of programs enacted.

The largest and most enduring federal assistance programs, launched in 1965, were Medicare, which pays for many of the medical costs of the elderly; and Medicaid, which aids poor people. The centerpiece of the War on Poverty was the Economic Opportunity Act of 1964, which created an Office of Economic Opportunity (OEO) to oversee a variety of community-based antipoverty programs. The OEO reflected a fragile consensus among policymakers that the best way to deal with poverty was not simply to raise the incomes of the poor but also to help them better themselves through education, job training, and community development. Central to the OEO's mission was the idea of "community action"—the participation of the poor in framing and administering the programs designed to help them.

The many far-reaching programs of the Great Society and War on Poverty had the support of the Federal Reserve and the Treasury in spite of the projected future costs of those programs. With the Vietnam War continuing and growing through this period, there was little resistance from Congress to increasing potential budget expenses. Funding was effortlessly provided by the Treasury and Federal Reserve to help the president and Congress provide more societal benefits to offset the public unrest over the expenses and military-personnel losses of the Vietnam War. It was easy for the president and Congress to buy votes with new programs to cure perceived societal problems, while continuing the unpopular Vietnam War.

The Kennedy-Johnson era set up a liberal renaissance that enlarged the Roosevelt "New Deal" programs that were implemented to help bring the country out of the Great Depression of the 1930s. Though there were differing opinions regarding the success of the New Deal programs, much credit was given to the philosophy of John Maynard Keynes. The Keynesian philosophy was cemented into the thinking of the Federal Reserve from that time on. It took the preparation for World War II spending and budget controls, in addition to major military spending, to bring the country out of the Depression. Although the Keynesian philosophy was at best marginally effective through most of the 1930s, it was given credit for the economy's recovery during and after the war. With the Fed using the Keynesian philosophy, and the enlarged programs of the Great Society and the War on Poverty, the country was set up for the inflationary and low-growth years of the 1970s.

Until the early 1970s, the United States and much of the international business world were dominated by the Bretton Woods Agreement. Prior to the end of World War II, 730 delegates from all forty-four Allied nations gathered at the Mount Washington Hotel in Bretton Woods, New Hampshire, United States, for what became known as the Bretton Woods Conference. The delegates deliberated from the first to the twenty-second of July 1944, and signed the Agreement on the final day. The agreement set up a system of rules, institutions, and procedures to regulate the international monetary system. The planners at Bretton Woods established the International Monetary Fund (IMF) and the International Bank for Reconstruction and Development (IBRD), which today is part of the World Bank Group. These organizations became operational in 1945 after a sufficient number of countries had ratified the agreement.

The chief features of the Bretton Woods system were an obligation for each country to adopt a monetary policy that maintained the exchange rate by tying its currency to the US dollar, and the ability of the IMF to bridge temporary imbalances of payments.

THE END OF BRETTON WOODS, AND INFLATION OF THE 1970S

In the late 1960s, it was apparent to the public that the juggernaut of economic growth was slowing down. It began to become visibly apparent in the early 1970s. The slower economy was due to Vietnam involvement and social disruptions from it and the Cold War. The United States grew increasingly dependent on oil imports from OPEC after US production peaked in 1970, resulting in oil supply shocks in 1973 and 1979. Stagflation gripped the nation, and the government experimented with wage and price controls under President Nixon. The Bretton Woods Agreement collapsed in 1971 and 1972, and President Nixon closed the gold window at the Federal Reserve, taking the United States entirely off the gold standard.

President Gerald Ford introduced the slogan "Whip Inflation Now" (WIN). In 1974, productivity shrunk by 1.5 percent, though it soon recovered. In 1976, Jimmy Carter won the presidency. Carter would later take much of the blame for the even more turbulent economic times to come, though some say circumstances were outside his control. Inflation continued to climb skyward. Productivity growth was small when it wasn't negative. Interest rates remained high, with the prime reaching 20 percent in January 1981. Art Buchwald quipped that 1980 would go down in history as the year when it was cheaper to borrow money from the Mafia than the local bank.

This period also saw the increased rise of the environmental and consumer movements. The government established new regulations and regulatory agencies such as the Occupational Safety and Health Administration, the Consumer Product Safety Commission, the Nuclear Regulatory Commission, and others. Although the Vietnam War ended in 1975, the addition of more regulatory agencies, continued military spending, and the increased cost of government financing led inflation to increase while confidence in Keynesian economics fell. A change in the Federal Reserve leadership and higher interest rates brought the economy back to reality and to lower rates of inflation. In spite of the obvious weakness in Keynesian economics and the end of the gold value that limited the quantity of fiat currency, the Federal Reserve and Congress failed to learn from the inflationary lessons of the 1970s.

In the early 1980s, the Federal Reserve managed interest rates to higher levels and was able to reduce inflation and stabilize the economy. Through the rest of the 1980s and into the first decades of the 2000s, the Federal Reserve has continued to manage interest rates to suit political purposes. The end of the Bretton Woods agreement in 1971 has made it easier to use the money supply to manage the interest-rate market. Instead of allowing the free market to set the interest rates of government bonds, the Federal Reserve can create more currency to purchase government bonds, and thus lower rates, when needed. The rationale for doing this, as is often stated, is "to avoid deflation" and the loss of value of capital assets as happened during the Depression. While avoiding deflation, the following booms and bust events happened to the country:

1. Market crashes such as the stock market crash of October 1987.
2. The Japanese real estate and market crash of 1991.
3. The emerging market bubbles and crashes of 1994 and 1997.
4. The LTCM crisis of 1998; the dotcom bubble burst in 2000.
5. The bubble leading to the depression from 2007 to the present.

There is no doubt that the congressional and political actions, along with Federal Reserve operations, have contributed to the turbulence that the US economy has experienced. Both political parties have been involved in using Federal Reserve funding to buy votes, which has contributed to the difficulties that the citizens of the United States have had to endure. The US federal budget deficit has been created by a combination of congressional actions that were funded by what were intended to be "flexible" Federal Reserve budget activities. In the hundred years of the Fed's existence—from its creation in 1913 to 2013—the total of all budget deficits equaled between fourteen and fifteen trillion dollars. Since the demise of Bretton Woods in 1971, the total of all budget deficits equaled nearly thirteen trillion dollars. The increase in the last forty years has accounted for 97 percent of all budget deficits in this country. The deficit is projected to grow to almost twenty trillion dollars over the next ten years.

The deficits that have developed over the years, and particularly since 1971, occurred basically because the Federal Reserve has acted in concert with Congress and the presidents to fund benefits that those politicians used to gain political office. The Federal Reserve and its board of major banks, while acting to "avoid deflation," have caused losses for US taxpayers in the form of inflation and higher taxes. They have now brought the financial system close to collapse. It has been easy for the Federal Reserve to fund federal programs by creating currency. The large banks' leaders, who do not have to work hard for a living, can thus help to buy votes from working citizens to keep those same citizens dependent on the central government.

THE SECOND GREAT DEPRESSION

The depression that started in 2007 has changed the outlook and future prospects for US citizens. The Fed's easy funding of government programs that started in the late 1960s has made many citizens dependent on Washington and government in general. The politics of Congress and the presidents that made it easier for home investment, coupled with the use and expansion of derivatives, set up the economy to suffer tremendous losses. Minimal restrictions on the means and methods of financing home ownership allowed too much risk for banks, homeowners, and the nation's taxpayers. Homebuyers and their lenders were encouraged to take on much risk by the Fed's policy of keeping rates low and credit easily available. Derivative bets on home financing have been estimated at forty to sixty times the value of the actual property values used by lenders. Political actions by Congress, the presidents, and the Federal Reserve all contributed to this economic disaster.

The impact of political errors, and Fed compliance in managing the national finance, has been devastating to citizen taxpayers. Some of the effects that the country has suffered are as follows:

1. Loss of individuals' values and freedom due to increased direction from Washington.
2. Loss of individual responsibility and independence due to dependence on Washington.
3. Decreased abilities of local and state governments to guide local economies.
4. Unlimited growth in size of local, state, individuals, and family budgets.
5. Growth of federal budget deficits without end.
6. Minimized and restricted use of local resources.
7. Unequal and unreasonable tax levels to fund growing government budgets.
8. Unlimited funding of international activities without benefit to the nation.
9. Limits on the capitalist, free-market business economy due to federal regulations.

10. Federal Reserve control of interest rates and pricing by avoiding the free market.
11. Inflexible federal regulations on labor and economic issues limiting free market actions.
12. Loss of commonsense justice in maintaining local and state legal order.
13. Victimless crimes unnecessarily overloading prisons and judicial authorities.
14. Increased cost of goods without a currency backed by a resource of market value.
15. Responsive commonsense government overruled by Washington.
16. Lost respect for God and other individuals, who have been replaced by Washington.

It has become obvious that the lack of leadership by government and the Federal Reserve has made it necessary that there be a major change in the philosophy and direction of the nation.

REBIRTH OF FREEDOM'S NATION WITH COMMONSENSE GOVERNMENT

COMMONSENSE ECONOMICS

Commonsense is a rational, logical way of thinking with regard to an issue, concern, or subject. What person would loan money to another who would not likely be able to pay him or her back? The United States had only a little over thirteen trillion dollars of deficits over one hundred years after the Federal Reserve was created. Over the last forty-one years (less than half the time) the United States generated over thirteen trillion dollars of deficits. By 2015, the US budget deficit will have expanded to at least $16.5 trillion. With balanced budgets, starting in 2015, it would take almost nineteen years to pay off the budget deficit, without even counting off-budget items that add tens of billions to the budget deficit.

It is unrealistic to believe that the US taxpayer—and certainly not foreign countries—will want to continue funding the US spending to "avoid deflation," as stated by the Federal Reserve chairman. Although the Keynesian monetary philosophy has been able to use deficit spending to resolve past recessions, it is unlikely that larger deficits will be able to pull the US economy out of the latest great depression. The Keynesian philosophy was unable to pull the economy back to positive growth with a high employment level from the 2008 bottom, and it does not appear to be likely in the future, as of 2014. Higher deficits with slow growth will mean rising interest rates for US Treasury bonds in future years. Rising interest rates will only contribute to increased budget deficits at a faster rate of real inflation, thus impacting US taxpayers, who must fund the US budget.

The Keynesian philosophy has been proven wrong in the 1929 and 2008 depressions. That philosophy has made it possible for the Federal Reserve to buy votes for presidents and congressional politicians who care more about buying votes with benefits than earning taxpayers' support. Unfortunately, both major political parties were involved in these actions. The founders of the United States showed that they believed that freedom of choice was a God-given right by placing emphasis on this in the Constitution and Bill of Rights. This made the US economy grow into a great power up to and until the early 1900s, when the Federal Reserve was created.

During the country's first 150 years, leaders avoided governance by the elite, as was present in Great Britain when it was ruled by the aristocracy and wealthy citizens. Yet when the country suffered through several banking panics in the 1800s, the same type of people who had been responsible for those panics chose to create a third central bank. That central bank, the Federal Reserve, was set up with a board of elite bank leaders nominated by the president and approved by Congress, thus assuring political influence. Over the years, the Federal Reserve gained more power over the economy. In 1971 it gained overwhelming power by its ability to create currency without a realistic value-backed free market and publicly available materials such as gold or silver.

Since the Federal Reserve was created in 1913, there have been many booms and busts in the economy. The two biggest booms in the "Roaring Twenties" and the 2006-to-2008 years led to the biggest busts. Both busts were caused by too-low interest rates and too much leverage for stocks and housing. In those cases and many others, the Federal Reserve had the opportunity to simply allow the free market to limit risk taken by investors. Instead of allowing the free market to raise interest rates to prevent potential busts, the Federal Reserve allowed politics to influence its actions, and it rode the popularity of temporary booms. The large banks benefit from booms and are somewhat harmed by recessions, as deposits and use of their services change accordingly. Considering the executives of the large banks are on the board of the Federal Reserve, it is easy to see why booms tend to be larger, and busts take a lot longer to end. It is easier to see why top executives of the large banks, and the chairmen of the Federal Reserve, have not served jail time for the busts. Perhaps it is because they are managing other people's money, and that the risks they allow are not accomplished with their own money. Both depressions were paid for by the taxpayers and by the depositors at their banks.

When the nation was founded, our leaders wanted freedom for individuals and markets that allowed individuals to take risks that benefitted them if they were successful in overcoming the challenges. What has happened over the last hundred years is that freedom has slowly been taken from the individual, making him or her dependent upon the national government. The obvious effect of this loss of freedom is how the country has suffered drastically higher budget deficits, particularly within the last forty-five years. These deficits were the result of drastically higher benefits given to the majority of citizens who were outside of the major source of taxes: the middle class. **The middle class has shrunk from 62 percent in 1970 to only 45 percent in 2013.**

It is also obvious that the largest increase in the deficit happened over the same period of time as the reduction in the middle class. The Federal Reserve, using its ability to create more fiat currency, has helped fund government programs that have taken freedom from the middle class to buy votes from and increase benefits for over 40 percent of the population. It was the middle class and able leaders who founded the country and set the standards that made it one of the leading nations in the world. It has been the Federal Reserve and unprincipled leaders who have taken freedom from the majority of taxpayers and made them more dependent upon the federal government. It does not make common sense to take from the major source of income for the country while reducing the benefits to that source, as any businessperson would understand.

COMMONSENSE ACTIONS TO REGAIN INDIVIDUAL FREEDOM

From the previous discussion, it is obvious that the power of the Federal Reserve must be limited in order to free the middle-class taxpayers. An audit by Congress of the Federal Reserve is necessary to determine how it should act to gain an improved economy. To date, the Federal Reserve has bought Treasury bonds with money that it created while paying almost no interest to taxpayers who have savings. The large banks that make up the Federal Reserve have used low-interest loans to pay off trillions of dollars of mortgage debt generated in 2008. Businesses needing loans to grow have been limited by banks regarding how much they can borrow, due to the banks' reluctance to take risks beyond their derivative losses. Had the Federal Reserve allowed the free market to work during 2008, the large banks would have separated housing loans from their customer savings, and taken losses on the housing loans in bankruptcy procedures. In the worst case, the Federal Reserve would go bankrupt, and its mistakes could be corrected in a new central bank. Since the past is the past, an audit by Congress can retroactively identify the errors in judgment made since 2008, so that corrections can be made in the future.

It is near impossible to understand how taxpaying citizens will continue to support Federal Reserve actions, for the following reasons:

1. It favors increasing the tax levels that they pay.
2. It devalues the money they take home with rising deficits and public debt.
3. It pays less than 1 percent to them on their savings.
4. It helped elect a socialist president by funding entitlement programs.
5. It has been unable to help reduce high unemployment and underemployment.
6. It provides low-cost loans to the lending institutions responsible for the 2008 depression.
7. It has provided no basis for the value of the national currency.

When the above items are considered, an audit and reorganization of the Federal Reserve would be the commonsense solution.

Simply auditing the Federal Reserve to reorganize it would only identify needed improvements. As previously pointed out regarding the increase in budget deficits since the end of Bretton Woods in 1971, the United States has become a debtor country. Pricing of goods in this country has depended upon the US dollar being recognized as the international reserve currency used for international transactions. International reserve currency status means that it is used for most of this country's foreign purchases, and has thus kept US citizens' prices low.

A return to using the value of gold for the basis of the currency would tie the value of the currency to the real world of publicly traded pricing of a historically recognized currency. The value of a currency would not be subject to politically devised measures of inflation, as has been done over the last twenty years. An individual would be able to determine the value of a good that was referenced to a known free-market price of whatever he or she was purchasing.

With the Federal Reserve unable to create currency without real-world support, it would not be able to buy Treasury bonds to keep this country's interest rates below a free-market rate. With true measures of inflation, Treasury interest rates would be subject to free-market levels and could not be kept below realistic international rates. The ability to finance its own government operations with a created currency—and the fact that the US dollar is the international reserve currency—have kept the price of US goods low. With realistic currency values for the US dollar, and lower use of the dollar for international transactions, the price of imported goods would rise. The inflation rates that the United States has been exporting to other countries would come home.

With realistic purchasing power of the dollar, interest rates would be based on the country's need to borrow from the countries that now mostly supply the country with basic necessities. With the extreme deficits that now exist and are growing, the cost of living in this country will rise as more currencies of other countries such as China, Russia, Europe, and India are used in international trade.

Another thing that would make common sense would be setting a limit on fractional reserve banking. As previously stated, federal regulations that loosened mortgage-lending standards, coupled with fractional reserves taken to extremes of forty to sixty, helped cause the current depression. This means that a bank or other lending institution would limit the amount that it could loan to a borrower by no more than a multiple of the reserves (or deposits) that it has in its possession.

In addition, this would mean that the central bank (Federal Reserve) would be limited in the amount that it could loan to member banks or the government. With the value of the currency dependent upon the market value of gold (or any publically traded real asset), the Federal Reserve would be limited in how much it could lend without obviously creating measurable inflation. Funding government expenses with created currency of no real value (fiat currency) would require government programs to be tied to the real world, as it is in balanced-budget states.

By limiting fractional reserve multipliers, the United States could function as it had for 150 years before the Great Depression, when country grew from birth to a great free-market industrial and business nation. With limits on multiples of reserves, the country—as well as most states—could generate balanced budgets that do not push loan payments out to future generations.

An area of contention from the first central bank to the present is the composition of the managing board. The current board is made up of regional bank representatives. In their early discussions about a central bank, many of the country's leaders believed that the central bank would favor only the elite and not help the common man. Nevertheless, the Federal Reserve was put together by the top bankers and those who did business with them. The board for the Federal Reserve should be composed of the most successful businesspeople of these times so that they have an understanding of what it takes to build, operate, and fund a business from the start. The Chairman of the Federal Reserve board should be elected by the board. Board members and the chairman should be approved by both houses of Congress, and are not beholden to the president or the Secretary of the Treasury. Terms of board members should be staggered so that it would take at least six years to completely change each position.

There could still be political influence on how the Federal Reserve operates, but the board members would more likely represent the total citizens of the country rather than the politics of a couple of politicians. With the Federal Reserve central bank managed by representative business leaders and decisions being made that guide the nation's economy, taxpaying citizens could have confidence in the economy's direction. Variations in the country's economy could still occur, but taxpayers will know choices were made with their interests in mind.

The desire to provide flexible funding for government could still be handled with a revised Federal Reserve. Tying the value of the currency to gold would provide a realistic value to the dollar and make it obvious when the amount of money in the public exceeded the quantity needed for transactions. Interest rates would be based upon what the finance market valued the dollar at and the purchaser's confidence in recovering the investment in the bond. The interest rate would depend upon how the purchaser valued the bond, not on what the central bank decided to pay for it with created fiat currency. Bond prices, and interest paid on those bonds, would be based upon a free-market transaction. In a free market, continued deficits would lower the value of Treasury bonds and drive interest rates up for the government and the public. The value of the dollar currency would depend upon comparison with other currencies on the international market. Each country's ability to finance its government operation would depend upon how each managed its internal finances. Once the United States got its finances in order and realistically valued, the dollar could rightfully deserve to claim the title of world reserve currency.

Since 1971, the finances of the United States have relied on its currency being the reserve currency used for commercial transactions around the world. The country has used its reserve currency status to finance its operations by bond purchases with reserves from other countries. Those purchases were made by countries knowing that the dollar was created without a realistic market-supported asset value. The 2008 depression generated many trillions of dollars of debt for major US financial institutions, some of which failed. Those that survived were saved from bankruptcy by loans and grants from the federal government, for which the Federal Reserve provided funding by using created currency.

The international markets have viewed the descending credit level and high deficits of the United States with concern. This has prompted moves by financially sound countries to begin making transactions without use of the US dollar or charging more dollars for goods bought for the US. Over the last few years, more international business transactions using currencies other than the dollar, and lower levels of purchases of US Treasury bonds, have caused interest rates to start rising. The Federal Reserve must be improved to get the country's finances in order so that the nation that was founded for individual freedom can again become "Freedom's Nation."

The increase of dependence on the federal government has taken the focus away from the original philosophy of the God-given right to individual freedom. As the federal central government grew more powerful due to increased benefits and accompanying regulations from the federal bureaucracy, the freedom of choice for individuals was diminished. Citizens focused more on following federal rules, and less on the Constitution that was created by Christians to give individuals their freedom.

The government that was intended to provide a just and orderly life for its citizens has become disorderly, with restrictions based upon political issues instead of general principles. There is a need for leaders who follow commonsense, logical thinking, instead of playing politics to gain support and votes from small, focused groups. With a review and reorganization of the Federal Reserve, individual citizens will be free to pursue their maximum potential for happiness in Freedom's Nation.

LEADERSHIP EFFORTS NEEDED AFTER 2016

FREEDOM'S NATION NEEDS

The leadership, to take this country back to the strength it developed over its first 150 years, will have to address a number of critical issues. Those issues are as follows:

1. Reorganization of the Federal Reserve central bank
2. Addressing the growing cost and size of entitlements
3. Regaining national budget control to reduce the national debt and future tax levels
4. Reorganizing the authorities and responsibilities of government
5. Developing simple and growth-supporting tax policies
6. Changing the nation's focus from international policeman to international trader

The country is in dire need of a new group of moral, honest leaders and citizens who desire to make the world a better place for all. **In a moral, honest, God-concerned world, the following would exist:**

1. **Congressional and presidential political candidates would not expect to buy votes with benefits.**
2. **Individuals would not expect benefits for something that they did not earn through their own efforts.**
3. **The Federal Reserve would not fund federal programs with a currency that had no realistic value.**

When this nation's founders earned the country's freedom from a strong Great Britain government, they sought freedom for the individual to make choices to gain his or her maximum God-given potential. Great Britain was a country governed by royalty and elite favorites of the rulers. In building rules and standards to govern the people in the new nation, the founders of the United States sought to avoid a too-strong or oppressive central government. The Constitution and Bill of Rights were written to guide the government in that direction. This country's government has moved away from its original intent and increasingly toward the very type of government that the founders feared. This has happened because of the greed of many citizens and the compliance of the Federal Reserve with benefitting a few at the expense of many.

An overpowering federal government has developed over the last fifty years. Strong federal government advocates are known as statists, yet the power has been taken from the states and from individuals. The statists have worked to increase the strength of the federal/central government by making many citizens dependent upon it for benefits. This is all too similar to the dependence that slaves had on their masters. Were it not for the Civil War and the Constitution, many citizens would not have the benefits of today, yet they have much of the dependence.

The United States must get back to the goals of freedom and independence that the wise founders desired for its citizens. Potential leaders must understand that everyone—like the early citizens of this country—wants to experience the joy of freedom and the ability to improve himself or herself. Reaching this goal will require many changes to our present-day situation.

One of the first issues that must be addressed is the importance of the individual. The individual must be able to make choices that benefit him or her, without the interference of government. Regulations are necessary, and order must be maintained to prevent physical injuries or personal property damage to others. The right to orderly freedom will allow and encourage a free market that values things in accordance with cost versus quantity of the item or action.

REORGANIZING THE FEDERAL RESERVE

As previously mentioned, the Keynesian economic philosophy has not worked well in all cases. It is common sense that a stable economy will allow the economy to grow at a pace that will coincide with the development of the government's individual citizens. A philosophy that distorts the free market by encouraging government to spend more than needed (deficits), and then must encourage reduced spending to discourage inflation, is not common sense. The Federal Reserve has allowed booms that caused inflation in the 1970s, the 1990s, and from 2005 to 2008. It was only in the 1980s, during one commonsense period, that this country regained a stable economy. In spite of this, the majority of Federal Reserve board members continue to believe in the Keynesian philosophy. It is only because of the ability of the Fed to fund congressional programs to help elect politicians that a realistic audit has been avoided.

An audit by Congress of the Federal Reserve is necessary for the government to ensure that the economy that the Fed manages is working as the original Congress wanted. The nation's founders wanted an economy that was able to avoid extremes. It will be necessary to audit the Federal Reserve as soon as possible, considering the damage done to the economy since 1971. There have been several attempts by Congress members to obtain an audit, yet politicians of both parties have resisted realistic oversight of what should be the role of Congress to manage the economy. Only a true and realistic audit can give the government a clear perspective on the central bank's management of the economy.

An audit of the Federal Reserve will show that management by a board of elite large banks has not resulted in decisions that benefit taxpaying citizens. The large banks, and those banks' chosen large customers, benefitted most from decisions made by the Federal Reserve Board. Politics to please elite, politically influential organizations appears to weigh heavily in decisions of the board. A reorganization of the central bank of this country should include the following actions:

1. The reinstatement of gold as the basis for valuing the currency.
2. Choice and approval of board members from the business community by Congress.

3. Setting a limit on required reserve levels for banks to avoid the possibility of bankruptcy.
4. Limiting derivative use and reserves used by financial operations for investments.
5. Using international market levels to value gold.
6. Limiting annual deficit levels increases, if they cannot be eliminated in twenty years.

Commonsense management of the nation's economy will result in removing the overwhelming power of Washington's federal government. The original thinking of placing more authority in the hands of states, local governments, and individuals has been changing since the creation of the Federal Reserve, the onset of the Great Depression, and the end of Bretton Woods in 1971. Slowly but surely, states, local governments, and individuals lost authority and responsibility. Today the federal Washington government has much more authority and responsibility than it had before the year 1900. The potential of each person, each community, and each state to progress their economies at the rate that best fits their local resources and abilities has been lost. Instead, each person, community, and state depends upon the federal government to provide regulations to tell them how to best please the dictates of Washington.

Since 1960, Congress has raised the debt ceiling seventy-eight times as the Federal Reserve helped fund the increased debts of the taxpaying citizens of the country. It is understandable that the taxpaying citizens have lost confidence in the current president, Congress, and the economy. Future leaders of the United States must reorganize the Federal Reserve to move authority and responsibility back to individuals, local communities, and states, and away from the federal government in Washington.

ENTITLEMENT MANAGEMENT CONTROL

Over the last eighty years, a major reason that the total budget deficit has grown is the collection of entitlement programs that provide benefits to residents of this country. Some of the programs, such as social security, were started during the Great Depression by Franklin Delano Roosevelt and have been expanding ever since. A major increase in these entitlement programs came about in the late 1960s with the Great Society and War on Poverty, which were launched to offset the growing public outcry over the Vietnam War. As previously pointed out, the largest federal budget deficits have developed since the end of the Bretton Woods Agreement in 1971. Many additions to entitlement programs were made by Congress in attempts to gain more votes of specific groups and extend congresspersons' times in office.

Many of these entitlement programs are in danger, in spite of required payroll taxes on individuals and businesses to fund them. Those citizens and businesses paying the taxes have a right to benefit according to the level of funds that they contributed. They should receive fair and equal benefits based upon how long they were enrolled in the programs. Payroll-funded federal programs have been experiencing shortfalls (deficits) between taxes paid and benefits paid out for several years. Part of the shortfall exists because benefit amounts depend upon a strategy of new enrollments in the programs, which help to pay the benefits of those members who have been in the programs for years. In some areas of business, programs that depend upon new growth for continuing payments are considered fraud and are known as Ponzi schemes. The danger in building deficits into these programs is that either the future benefits will need to be reduced, or payroll taxes will have to increase.

Many working people who are involved in guaranteed pension plans have long been satisfied with expecting the pension amount that is set by their contribution and time of enrollment in the plan. Those pension-entitled workers must either continue with that employer and plan or contribute to a personal savings plan of their own. Private pension plans are often funded by a business operation and/or contributions made by those enrolled in the plans, or both. It is common sense for benefits to be based upon the contributions made to the plan, and how long the worker was part of the plan. Benefits paid by private pension plans do not require taxpayer funds, though workers in those plans will still pay government-required taxes.

Federal-government entitlement programs do require taxpayer funds in order to provide benefits. In order to avoid reducing or eliminating benefits to these programs, or increasing taxes to pay for them, new leaders will need to address how to decrease ongoing pension deficits. This can be done with some commonsense actions:

1. Require any individuals who receive benefits from an entitlement program to have been enrolled (paid taxes or made contributions) in the program.
2. Require any individuals who receive benefits from an entitlement program to either be US citizens or minor children of citizens.
3. Base benefit levels for individuals on the amount that they or their employer has contributed in their name, and for their time enrolled in the program.
4. Limit the maximum benefit for individuals based upon the amount that they or their employer have contributed in their name, based on a limited time of their enrollment in the program.
5. Entitlement programs not funded by the federal government should be funded by state, county, or local government, and should be set according to need and available funds.
6. Contributions to state, county, and local government programs should be funded by taxes and fees set by those jurisdictions.

Whether an entitlement program is overseen by a federal, state, or local government, there will be a need to provide aid to individuals who experience unplanned occurrences that reduce income or increase expenses. There will be a need for supplemental income for some period of time until the person can adjust his or her living conditions. To gain control of budgets, government must limit the time and funding for such instances. In a country that focuses on freedom of the individual, the individuals involved in crisis situations must take responsibility for improving their circumstances. Government funds to aid crisis situations must come from excess tax or service revenue not used for normal capital or operating expenses.

Citizens' benefits for state, county, or local governments that provide aid or reduce risk are best set in an area or region that is most familiar with the resources and local environments there. The citizens in government areas served by more familiar and known governments will be best served by governments that can make the best use of their local jurisdictions' resources and abilities. With more local responsibility and authority, common sense can be used to gain better results than a one-size-fits-all program administered by a centralized government that is unfamiliar with an area's resources.

Reductions in entitlement programs will help stem some of the continuing rise in the federal budget deficit. Establishing a reasonable and commonsense operation of the Federal Reserve can help Congress and the federal administration develop a commonsense basis for budgets. Basing budgets on, and financing budgets with, a currency that is realistic would improve the process of achieving a reasonable balanced budget. The growing national deficit could at least be slowed to save key programs that give the citizens of this country the benefit of gaining more from the investments that it makes in those programs. For non-accountants, this means that citizens will get positive returns on investments made by the federal government with citizens' tax dollars.

It should be evident to most citizen taxpayers that, with the tremendous growth in the deficit in recent years, the federal government has invested poorly. Results such as high unemployment, high underemployment, a rising cost of living, a shrinking middle class, and growing debt have shown little positive direction. Future Congressional and presidential leaders must address gaining control of the federal budget to ensure that federal government programs, and the government itself, do not go bankrupt. Without improved leadership, the present and future generations will lose the opportunity to regain the power that "Freedom's Nation" knew during its first 150 years.

BUDGET CONTROL TO REDUCE DEBT AND FUTURE TAX LEVELS

Although it will be very difficult to gain control of the federal budget, due to the prevailing attitude and history over the last forty-five years, a new concept for budgeting will need to be used. As just mentioned, the budgeting and investment concept of return on investment can be used. What this means is that an investment of time, money, or resources should provide a return or benefit that is positive. The higher the return or positive number of time, money, or resource (or a combination of any or all of these), the higher the benefit for the program or action. For a government budget, this means that the people paying the taxes or fees will benefit indirectly from how their taxes or fees are used. This is not a highly technical concept, so even a government politician should be able to grasp it.

Using a commonsense method of budget development of return on investment will allow us to reach a balanced budget within six years. This is a period that can coincide with the election of new congressional leaders, and bring in new leaders who can apply common sense to replace existing deficit-growing programs. The ultimate goal of responsible federal government leaders should be to gain control of the annual budget, so that debt can be managed realistically.

If the national debt becomes too large, confidence in the United States will fall. The country's trading partners will not purchase the bonds that fund government expenses. Reduction in the sale of, and demand for, US bonds will drive interest rates up, increase growth of the federal debt, and endanger the reserve status of the nation's currency. Loss of reserve status in financing the government's business will drive up prices of goods for US consumers. Rising interest rates, rising federal debt, and rising prices will move the country into an inflationary recession. With higher interest rates on federal debt, tax rates will either have to rise to maintain service levels for citizens, or benefit programs will have to be reduced. If citizens think that their situation of high unemployment and negative future prospects are bad now, the situation could become worse in a short time of only a few months.

The national debt and continuing debasement of the world's reserve currency have generated much resentment and loss of respect from those countries that have managed their own finances responsibly. Many countries that the United States relies upon for supplies of goods and raw materials have seen their cost of living increase, while this country enjoys lower costs and high standards of living.

The national debt will be over $16 trillion by the end of September 2014, not counting off-budget items. With rising interest rates, the interest on this debt will only make deficits and the national debt grow faster. The rapid growth of US debt and deficits has caused former purchasers of treasury bonds to shrink the quantity and terms of their purchases. Those countries that have the finances to purchase bonds have little confidence that the United States will be able to pay them enough interest to offset its inflated cost of living. Although the federal government releases inflation numbers that fail to include food and energy data, it does not make sense that the rate of inflation is less than 1 or 2 percent. It is very unlikely that people in this country or other countries do not eat or use energy. With high and rising debt, the future direct and interest costs of government will increase the obligations of future workers. This will only reduce workers' standard of living, as less income will be available for basic needs. New leadership for the United States must stop the continuation of deficits and the escalation of the national debt.

Debt-reduction measures must start with the budget for 2015. It is possible to reduce the national debt to zero in thirty years, and free future generations from reductions in their standard of living, by focusing actions in several key budget areas:

1. Begin balancing the federal budget in year one, including all off-budget items, to ensure there are no hidden budget costs, and use realistic accounting.
2. Finance required asset purchases over no more than twenty years, including principal and interest in budgets.

3. Sell all nonstrategic federally owned businesses' or services' assets to pay down debt.
4. Reduce or write down the debt principal by 5 percent per year for the first five years.
5. Pay a maximum interest rate of 4 percent per year on the total remaining principal of the debt.
6. Include all principal and interest in the annual budget.

All of these actions can be implemented by moral, responsible leaders who want a national government that performs in the interest of taxpaying citizens. It will be a challenge to convince many entitled voters that these changes will be needed, after over forty years of dependence upon the federal government.

Although balancing the budget in the first year would be very difficult, there must be some effort to reduce the enormous budget deficits that have become normal in the last few years. Without some effort, the purchasers of Treasury bonds will reduce their purchases and cause interest rates to increase. With higher interest rates on the country's debt, the total debt will increase at a faster pace. The reliability and honesty of the current data on inflation, GDP, and employment are not considered to be realistic because of the actual cost of food and energy, high unemployment, and high underemployment. An effort to balance the budget by reducing some programs' expenditures will provide some credibility to the budgeting process.

By auditing and identifying improvements to the Federal Reserve's operation, needed changes can be implemented. The continued use of Keynesian philosophy in funding government budgets has shown a disregard for taxpayers' welfare. Encouraging deficit spending by the federal government in order to repair the damage done by lax loan and interest rate standards with policies that encourage the same does not make sense. Continued creation of more currency that has no real value, except in hope, has required the establishment of false federal inflation measures to hide real values. The impact on the average citizen has been a reduced standard of living on take-home pay levels, as shown by the reduction of the number of people in the middle-income class. Reorganization of the Federal Reserve can bring the budget back under the control of people who have the interests of taxpaying citizens in mind, instead of the interests of leaders of large financial organizations. Gaining control of the budget and addressing reduction of the national debt can bring back the respect and strength of the country to ensure future growth for freedom's nation.

REORGANIZING THE AUTHORITY AND RESPONSIBILITIES OF GOVERNMENT

The present situation in government is one in which the federal government based in Washington dominates the thinking and responsibilities of individuals, states, counties, and local governments. The increase in activity of the federal government and federal regulatory agencies has generated a vast number of complicated regulations through the many federal programs that were started during the last forty-five years. Along with actual program legislative details, there have been many regulatory rules and regulations implemented by agencies within HUD, DOD, DOE, DOT, and other departments. As the federal government has increased its rules and regulations, it has required more responsibility from state, county, and local governments. As the responsibilities for administration have been pushed down to the state, county, and local governments, the authority of the federal government departments and agencies over lower-level governments has been maintained. This is not what the original leaders of this country intended.

As mentioned in my history of the early years of the United States, the intent of the Constitution and Bill of Rights was to give more freedom to individuals, states, and lower-level governments. The founding fathers wanted the citizens of this country to achieve satisfaction and happiness via the greatest use of their talents. The founders realized that, since the colonies and states had different resources, there could not be a central, supreme power in the form of a single government. The founding fathers had experienced the rule of a single overpowering government while under the rule of Great Britain. Although individuals would be free to maximize their capabilities, there would still need to be a government to maintain order and avoid harm from acts against others.

The founding fathers came from a Christian country and were knowledgeable of the laws of the church known as the Ten Commandments. Although those laws were not part of the Constitution or Bill of Rights, the country's leaders ensured that the standards that they set did not violate the Ten Commandments. According to the Declaration of Independence, freedom of the individual allowed citizens to follow any and all religions, even allowing them not to adopt a religion.

It is common sense that government should be most effective if its responsibilities and authority were centered closest to the individual. The resources available to an individual are those that are also closest to the individual. If that individual is governed by some political body, it also makes sense that he or she knows the individuals and resources within that body of government. It is also common sense that the level of government should be close to and knowledgeable of the resources, including the individuals, for which the governing body will be responsible. This level of government would be a local government such as a county or city. Taking this thinking forward, it is also makes common sense for the level of government overseeing local governments to be close to, and more knowledgeable of, the local resources and individuals in local areas.

In recent years, public opinion of both the president and Congress has been low. It is very likely that people feel that politicians are out of touch with the issues that are important to them. It is not possible to have a centralized method of government that attempts to make one size fit all. With each area of the country being different due to its different resources, people, and culture, it does not make sense to set laws, rules, and regulations that apply the same way to all areas. This has retarded and restricted growth of local economies that need an orderly government that encourages the best use of local resources. Growth is most possible when local, regional businesses are able to benefit from the land, transportation choices, weather, skills and abilities of local people, culture, and needed goods or services. With the federal government dominating the laws, rules, and regulations everywhere, it is no wonder that the economy has grown more slowly and that unemployment has been higher than it should be. The responsibilities and authorities of the levels of government must be reordered in order to improve the economy of all areas of the country.

The first step in reorganizing levels of government should focus on the highest degree of participation of individuals in the operations of businesses and government. This, of course, would mean the local community level. There, local resources are most obvious to individuals so they can make the best decisions regarding occupations, businesses, and services. There, local citizens would be familiar with the abilities and personal qualities of local politicians. Although limiting representation in government to only known, resident candidates could lead to inadequate local leadership, it is the choice that will be most acceptable to government operations in the long run. The issues of poor growth and improvement in the economy are much less likely to be huge issues where those in charge of regulation can make the best use of local assets.

The local community governments should have responsibility and authority over those functions that are particularly used or provided in the native area. This means that the local government should manage functions such as fire and police protection; regulation or operation of utilities (water, sewer, electricity, and natural gas); zoning for property use or development; streets, sidewalks and transportation; parks; schools; and building standards. Those functions should only be limited to local cases, and only overruled by a higher level of government that is limited from interfering in lower levels of government.

Under no cases should individual constitutional rights or freedoms be limited by a higher level of government. All of these functions are well suited to satisfying the needs of local community residents and taxpayers. In the case where local leaders are unable to satisfy the needs of the community, it is easiest to change representation and direction of operations. As originally intended by the founding fathers, the government at this level can provide the best opportunity for individuals, their families, and local businesses to grow and improve.

The state level of government is responsible for, and has authority over, a larger area than the local government. County governments can be classified as local, with the only difference being the size of the area served by that government. Many of the same functions listed for local governments will also apply to county governments. The state level of government has the advantage of assessing the successes or shortcomings of local governments and their use of resources. The state can appraise the progress of local governments to see if aid from, or coordination with, the state can help improve or remedy any challenges that local governments experience. Coordination of actions between local governments can help ensure the best uses of resources common to local government areas. Competition between and among local governments can be harmonized to provide positive results for all parties. The state can thus ensure that the assets within the state are developed to deliver the best results for economic growth.

It is the state's role to fully exploit the various natural or developed resources within its boundaries. At the same time, the state should work with local governments to ensure that growth in their economies contributes to the state's economy. It is important for the state government to minimize the negative influences of national or federal rules and regulations on local governments and individuals within them. Rules and regulations at the state level should complement local governments and individuals within them.

When the US government was being formed, the size and power of the national government were intended to be limited. More responsibility and authority was delegated to the states, so that they could each make best use of their natural resources. The role of the central government was limited to coordinating activities between and among the states. This was evident in the first cabinet of President George Washington. Washington had but four cabinet members:

1. Secretary of State
2. Secretary of Treasury
3. Secretary of War
4. Attorney General

In 1902, Theodore Roosevelt, a president who was considered a progressive, had only nine cabinet members:

1. Secretary of State
2. Secretary of Treasury
3. Secretary of War
4. Attorney General
5. Postmaster General
6. Secretary of the Navy
7. Secretary of the Interior
8. Secretary of Agriculture
9. Secretary of Commerce and Labor

In 2013, under the current president, Barack Obama, there are now fifteen cabinet members:

1. Secretary of State John Kerry
2. Secretary of the Treasury Jacob Lew
3. Secretary of Defense Chuck Hagel
4. Attorney General Eric Holder
5. Secretary of the Interior Sally Jewell
6. Secretary of Agriculture Tom J. Vilsack
7. Secretary of Commerce Penny Pritzker
8. Secretary of Labor Thomas E. Perez
9. Secretary of Health and Human Services Sylvia Burwell
10. Secretary of Housing and Urban Development Shaun Donovan
11. Secretary of Transportation Anthony Foxx
12. Secretary of Energy Ernest Moniz
13. Secretary of Education Arne Duncan
14. Secretary of Veterans Affairs Eric Shinseki
15. Secretary of Homeland Security Janet Napolitano

As can be seen by the growth in the number of the president's cabinet members, the growth in the federal government did not follow the common sense that was present in 1901 under Theodore Roosevelt. In fact, with today's advanced communication methods, there is little need for a postmaster general. Written messages are adequately handled by privately operated mail services, while the use of the Internet has reduced the time involved in many communications.

Of the other departments or cabinets under President Roosevelt, at least eight can be managed better by local and state governments. The Departments of the Interior and Agriculture could also have many of their functions better handled by the states. There is little reason for a one-size-fits-all program of rules and regulations for federally owned assets of a government to be managed by the bureaucracy in Washington, when each state and locality has uniquely different assets and resources. The same can be said for managing the agricultural assets that are uniquely different in each state. Thus, the Departments of the Interior and Agriculture would be limited to oversight and coordination, and direct authority would be limited to federally owned assets only. Taking this into consideration, commonsense management and administration could easily be done through six national departments:

1. Secretary of State
2. Secretary of Treasury
3. Secretary of Defense
4. Attorney General
5. Secretary of the Interior
6. Secretary of Agriculture

With the individual citizen given the freedom that was authorized by the Constitution and Bill of Rights, the nation can regain the strength and growth that it enjoyed before the Federal Reserve was created. Reorganizing the functions of government levels will remove the frustration that businesses and individuals have had with the dominating, complicated, and hard-to-understand government for the last forty-five years. Levels of government that are appropriate for each geographic and resource area will mean that economic potential will be gained for each community and state, and the nation as a whole. The negative results of a centralized government with one-size-fits-all rules and regulations will be replaced with leadership that places emphasis on maximizing the freedom, capabilities, and promise of individuals. More citizens will be able to realize the potential for happiness that the founders of this country intended for them.

DEVELOPING SIMPLE, GROWTH-SUPPORTING TAX POLICIES

No governing body can operate without a source of income or revenue. Under the dominating central government that evolved over the last century, more income was needed to gain votes by providing entitlements to voters. Much voter support was obtained by providing more benefits to each of many limited groups of citizens.

Although high-income individuals do not require more than basic food, shelter, and health care, it has been the policy of the federal government to increase tax levels as incomes grew. This has penalized the most successful people for working harder and working smarter than others. At the same time, benefits were given to those people who avoided working hard or were not successful at creating a business or providing work for others. Most citizens believe that some help should be given to those who have a hard time finding enough work to provide for themselves and their families.

In a country that was founded based on freedom of the individual, most citizens will admit that it is up to the individual to find work to provide for himself or herself. It is simply a matter of personal desire as to what will satisfy each individual to provide for himself or herself. A free person can change his or her requirements to best suit himself or herself as needed. Common sense tells you that income transfer from one person to another should be based upon the decision of the contributor, not the recipient—and definitely not by a mandate from government. When a government does have to intervene, the extent of aid or help should be determined by the majority of those whose funds must be contributed.

Governments generate expenses when they provide services for their citizens. All citizens cost the government for serving them, yet there are many who only pay sales taxes for goods and services, while over 40 percent pay no income or property tax. Citizens who receive the benefits of fire and police protection; travel on streets, highways, and sidewalks; use parks; receive sewer, water, telephone, and energy utility service; and benefits from zoning and property regulation cost the government money. The federal government provides a social security program and Medicare and Medicaid benefits to many people who get more out of those programs than they ever paid into them. Unemployment payments are paid to some who receive them longer than they have ever worked. Yet, with many receiving benefits from the federal government, there are many not paying taxes into it. As previously mentioned in the section on budget and deficit management, control of spending on entitlements must be accomplished. This can be done by simply placing commonsense limits on payouts.

Management of federal spending must be coordinated with common-sense tax policies to ensure that adequate income tax is generated for continuation of government benefit programs. Those tax policies will need to supply incentives to generate higher income from economic growth that will increase future revenue. Because the purpose of the guidelines of the Constitution and Bill of Rights was to free the individual citizen to realize his or her potential, the government's tax policy should do the same. The tax level of each taxpayer should reasonably be based upon whether he or she chooses to participate (enroll) in federal government benefit programs. If a taxpaying citizen chooses to participate in federal benefit programs, he or she will pay a flat (say, 20 percent) income tax. If an individual decides not to participate in federal benefit programs such as social security, Medicare, or Medicaid, he or she will pay a flat (say, 10 percent) income tax. Those who decide not to participate in federal benefit programs will receive up to a flat (say, 10 percent) deduction from their income before being subject to tax.

Businesses and corporations would be subject to the same guidelines. A business that chooses to provide a guaranteed retirement and health plan will pay a flat (say, 10 percent) tax on earnings, and can deduct up to a flat (say, 10 percent) tax on its earnings. A business that chooses not to provide a guaranteed retirement and health plan for its employees will pay a flat (say, 20 percent) tax on earnings. The tax policies for individuals and business or corporate taxes would be as follows:

Individual Taxes

10 percent income tax, if choosing to forgo federal benefits

20 percent income tax, if choosing to accept federal benefits

Up to 10 percent income tax deduction for personal savings plan while forgoing benefits

Business/Corporate Taxes
10 percent income tax, if choosing to fund a guaranteed retirement and health plan

20 percent income tax, if choosing not to fund a guaranteed retirement and health plan

Up to 10 percent income tax deduction for flexible benefits for workers while funding a guaranteed retirement and health plan

Individuals and businesses will still be able to deduct business expenses from their earnings, per IRS business-expense guidelines. With clear and simple tax policies, both corporate and individual tax levels will present adequate incentives for economic growth that will result in growth of income and opportunities for citizen taxpayers.

If and when federal budgets can approach being balanced, the challenge will be getting the benefit program funds to states and local governments. It makes sense that state and local governments can best determine the level of benefits needed, to afford what beneficiaries need to supply basic needs in their areas. The administration of federal benefits will be managed better by state and local governments, which really know the environments in which those benefits are distributed.

The federal government cannot be in charge of all taxes because it does not make common sense for an unfamiliar centralized government to know the environments that impact the ability to pay and use taxes. Because the national government should be limited to (reality-based) six departments that apply only to national issues, it is best that state and local governments most familiar with their environments and issues should management them.

At the state and local levels, taxes are mostly on property and sales of goods and services. Federal import taxes that only apply to the federal government should be revised to distribute import taxes to the states that receive goods or services. State and local governments also receive income from charges for services that they supply to individuals and businesses within their jurisdictions. Most well-run state and local governments maintain balanced budgets, with only realistic short-term (less than twenty years) financing of major asset investments.

With balanced budgets at state and local government levels, tax policies are a matter for the respective governments. Most government activities that impact the individual taxpaying citizen will be managed and administered at the local level. It is common sense that most property taxes and most sales taxes (say, two-thirds) will be administered by the local government. Because the state oversees and coordinates local government operations, it also makes sense that the state claims a significant part (say, one-third) of the property and sales taxes. Both governments should legally be able to charge to cover their costs for whatever services or permits they perform.

Tax policies at the state and local levels should be set to give the individual taxpayer the most freedom to choose what is best for him or her. Both state and local governments will need taxes and revenues to provide services to their citizens. These governments generally operate with balanced budgets for their own purposes.

With individual rights and freedoms given the highest priority, it makes common sense that state and local governments operate independently of the federal government. Under current operating procedures, state and local governments, like many individual citizens, depend upon funds passed down to them to help balance their budgets. If the main focus of government—whether central, state, or local—is the individual right of freedom of choice, states or local governments should not depend upon requirements of the central governments for funds. State and local governments should have the option of adapting federal government rules and regulations to best fit their local conditions. Growth and improvement of the nation's economy must start with the individual citizen, and pass through local and state economies to the nation as whole. Tax policies at the local level can be set as follows:

<u>Individual Income Taxes for Each State</u>
0 percent tax level on income
0 to 10 percent tax level on income
0 to 5 percent deduction from income for personal savings plans
<u>Corporate and Business Income Taxes for Each State</u>
0 percent tax level on income
0 to 10 percent tax level on income without a guaranteed retirement and health plan

0 to 5 percent deduction for a managed savings plan offered to employees

Property Taxes

.70 percent to 4 percent (varies) assessed on property value

66 percent of taxes collected and received by local government

33 percent of taxes received by state government from local government taxing authorities

Sales Taxes

0 to 7.5 percent state sales tax, with local tax added to the state tax level

0 to 2.0 percent local sales tax collected at local level and transmitted to the state

66 percent of tax collected and received at the local government level

33 percent of tax received at the state level from the local government

Local and state fees and charges for services

Charges set for actual cost of services provided

The individual taxpaying citizen is the most important participant in governments and their respective economies. With a tax policy that takes citizens' funds in order to serve them, it is common sense that those respective governments' tax policies encourage growth and improvement of individuals. With individual freedom of choice and the ability to use one's funds to improve one's future, the tax policies of state and local governments will naturally encourage more opportunities for individuals and businesses. As the prospects for each person improves, the opportunities for businesses that serve those people will improve. As local government economies improve, the state government economies will improve. State governments' improvements will then improve the nation's economy. With the above tax rates and policies boosting individuals, local governments, and state governments, the country will improve. The frustration of a controlled, restrictive federal government will be avoided, and people and businesses using free choice will realize their ultimate potential.

TURNING THE NATION'S FOCUS FROM INTERNATIONAL POLICEMAN TO INTERNATIONAL TRADER

From the country's birth and for its first 150 years, the US economy was supported by manufacturing and trade with other countries. Participation in World War I and II required a strong buildup of the military industry, which established the United States as a major force in international activities. Development of military bases in European countries and in Asian countries during and after World War II established the United States as a force in international affairs. Fear of the spread of communism caused continuing military obligations that continue to the present day.

The strength of the country's industry, along with its strong finances, made it possible for it to change its focus from international trade and supplying others to one of consuming the products of others. The Korean War and Vietnam War established the United States as a more aggressive force in international military activities. The finances of the United States were strong enough in the late 1960s that it was able to expand benefits to its citizens as it became more involved in the Vietnam War. When President Nixon dropped gold support for the dollar in 1971, the Federal Reserve was able to create (print) as many dollars as it needed to fund federal government programs.

In the late 1960s and into the 1970s, the United States changed from a nation of individual freedoms with strong manufacturing and trading activities to a consumer dependent upon other countries for supplies as well as finances. The United States has, literally, hundreds of military bases in over 120 countries. This commitment is greater than that of any other country, and equipping and maintaining this military presence creates great expenses. With continued activities in the Middle East in addition to the other foreign bases, the country's budget has expanded by many trillions since 1971. At the same time that the country spends much of its budget on military activities, the remainder of a rapidly growing budget is also used to maintain many of the benefit programs that were implemented beginning in 1968. It is likely that the total national budget will be over $16 trillion by October 2014. In 1970, the national debt was approximately $1 trillion.

Much of the growth in the national debt was accumulated during the last ten years by military engagements in the Middle East, while benefits for citizens grew because of weak economic activity from the "second great depression" of 2008. As weak economic conditions have contributed to higher federal debts and a significant increase in the national debt, confidence in the financial strength of the United States has fallen. Funding by the sale of Treasury bonds to foreign countries has caused ten- and thirty-year bond interest rates to rise. This means that the Federal Reserve has needed to print more dollars in order to purchase Treasury bonds to keep interest rates from rising to levels dangerous for the economy. The weak economy and national debt rising to a high (and growing) level has endangered the continued use of the US dollar as the world reserve currency for international business transactions.

The United States must maintain the ability to defend the country and its citizens from harm from other countries or organizations from other countries. Defense of the United States does not require defense of all of the countries in which the country has military bases. A gradual withdrawal from commitments other than defense of this country will be necessary.

With commonsense leadership and sensible management of the US budget to regain freedom for individuals and businesses, it is possible to regain trading activities that made the nation grow during the first 150 years. With growth in international trade, the ills of high unemployment, high underemployment, and inflation through inefficiency can be eliminated.

It has taken over forty years for this country to get to this point, so it will take many years and better leadership to effect a remedy. With more emphasis on trade with other countries, the interactions of non-defense military activities will improve relations with other countries. Activities of "Freedom's Nation" will increase the international image and reputation of the United States and improve trade. The demonstration of capitalism, rather than militarism, will show the world how to grow peacefully and prosperously.

IMPROVING THE NATION'S FREEDOM WITH NEW LEADERSHIP

NEW LEADERSHIP ACTIONS

Beyond the year 2016, new leadership for the United States will need to make significant changes to the way that the current statist, dominant central government works. Changes already mentioned in previous chapters are as follows:

1. Reviving the culture of individual freedom, and moving back to a constitutionally based government that supports a free market with a gold-backed currency.
2. Auditing and reorganizing the Federal Reserve to provide a taxpayer and citizen management board to replace oversight by the large financial organizations and elites now present.
3. Gaining control over growing entitlement programs that will fail those who depend on them in the near future as those programs become broke.
4. Reordering the levels of government to best serve tax-paying individuals, so that governments can best use local resources to reach their potential.
5. Simplifying tax policies and offering new ones that encourage growth of individuals and businesses so that they can use their freedom of choice to improve the economy.
6. Reviving freedom's nation by reducing and eliminating the national debt to salvage the possible loss of benefit from having the world's reserve currency.

Changing from the country's current thinking, where everybody is on his or her own and depends upon the government, to a country of liberty, freedom, and personal responsibility will take years. The nation has become a slave to government over the last forty-five years. The Constitution and Bill of Rights have lost authority while politics, focusing on specific voting blocs, has turned ordinary citizens into members of special interest groups. Responsibility and respect for self and others has been replaced by a concentration on envy of success and greed. Moral, honest, and responsible citizens have lost their commonsense thinking and ability to use the freedom that God gave them, instead becoming dependent upon federal government programs. Poor leadership by some of the country's governments has sacrificed the future of the nation and the very programs that many now depend upon. The direction in which the country is headed can be seen as interest rates rise, while the economy lags and the middle class shrinks.

New and better leaders must improve government to resurrect freedom's nation according to following schedule and actions:

PROGRESS TO FREEDOM'S NATION

1. **National Election in 2016**
2. **Implementing Commonsense Government to Audit the Federal Reserve**
3. **Auditing and Reorganizing of the Federal Reserve System**
4. **Implementing Freedom of the Individual at National Level**
5. **Implementing Revival of Freedom of Choice and Free Markets**
6. **Changing Government Finance Philosophy to Balance Budgets**
7. **Reorganizing Levels of Government to be Efficient and Effective**
8. **Balancing Government Budgets**
9. **Implementing Government Taxes for Growth and Progress**
10. **Changing Government Level Legal Systems for Order and Progress**

FREEDOM OF CHOICE BY LAW

With new leadership in the three branches of government, the guidelines for all levels of government will concentrate on the importance of individual freedom without harm to others. The Constitution and Bill of Rights will be followed by all, even at the local level of government. This will give each citizen the ability to choose freely how he or she can act, without committing unjust harm to others. Harm should be defined as that which causes measurable physical or property damage to another person or group of people. As intended by the nation's founders, each person in the country will have the opportunity to live up to his or her potential. With each person able to make the most of his or her abilities and resources, the prospect of local governments, state governments, and, finally, the nation for reaching the intended level of success will be realized.

The frustration and anger that citizens have experienced with the US federal government will be removed. The restrictions of detailed federal regulations that mandated how each citizen was required to act will be deleted from prosecution. The order that was proposed by the Constitution and Bill of Rights will be implemented by responsible individual citizens without prejudice toward any other individual or group of individuals. The politics of special groups, special treatments, and special remedies for ills or risks will be replaced by commonsense actions that will be fairly and justly accepted by all. The biased rules and regulations that have been enacted by irresponsible government representatives and legal authorities to gain votes in elections will be replaced by rational, logical regulations.

The new leaders of the central government will enact a law that makes all governments—from the central to local government level—follow the Constitution and Bill of Rights as intended in the Declaration of Independence:

"We hold these truths to be self-evident, that all men are created equal, that they are endowed by their Creator with certain unalienable rights. That among these are Life, Liberty, and the pursuit of Happiness."

Honest, responsible leaders will cast aside the recent interpretation of equality by socialist, Marxist politicians. There has been an attempt to use government to lump all citizens into a single class of subservient followers of a few socialist, statist leaders. It will require years to undo what has developed over the last forty-five years. The details added by federal bureaucrats—which added time and people required for regulatory compliance—must be rewritten to work at state and local government levels. At state and local levels, more rational and reasonable measures can be set that will apply to local area conditions and resources.

The transformation of the federal government, and reorganization of the levels of government and how they interact, will not only change people's opinions of government but will also change the results that are produced by government. The growth of the United States, with all of its vast, different resources of minerals, geographies, and creative individuals, can be revived as each person is able to seek and experience his or her potential. Citizens can realize opportunities to gain employment and as much of their desired functions in life as possible. With all people able to realize their potential, the nation will be able to regain its place as the leading industrial nation and ensure the identity of the world's reserve currency.

RETURN OF FREE MARKETS

The independent Federal Reserve has managed to gain control of the US economy and influence the central banks of Europe and Japan. By gaining control over the creation of currency and interest rates on government spending, the Federal Reserve has avoided and ignored the free and open markets that are governed by supply and demand. When a central bank such as the Federal Reserve literally prints new currency (the dollar) without any real backing or support to purchase Treasury bonds, it basically finances an operation without any value exchanged. Financing bonds by using created currency makes it easier and more flexible to pay federal government expenses; however, it creates a distorted market in the economy.

Purchasing Treasury bonds with funds of no real value has allowed the Federal Reserve to keep interest rates lower than what an open market would set. The low interest rates allow lending institutions to loan money to businesses at levels below what is needed to create (build) products or assets (homes) at costs below what an open market would warrant. Assets such as home mortgages are then priced below what buyers are able to pay for them. This means that the product, a home, is priced below what a citizen can pay for it over the length or term of the mortgage. When low prices and low financing costs creates excess demand for an asset such as a home, a correction to the normal market will occur, causing prices of that asset to fall.

Low-interest-rate financing for builders and home buyers created a booming home market because financing eliminated risks for home builders, home buyers, and home mortgage companies. The price of homes rose over a period of years with low risk to builders, buyers, and finance companies, until open-market prices reached high levels beyond the realistic normal level. The correction of market prices back to a normal level created a bust (a drop in price) in the housing market. If this happens for some length of time with other assets, this would be considered a recession. Of course, the Federal Reserve considers lowered prices of assets to be deflation. They believe that it is their responsibility to avoid deflation. They avoid deflation by decreasing the costs of assets by keeping rates below the free market level. Considering all of the above, the Federal Reserve creates money to keep interest rates low, to create oversupply (or booms), which then lead to busted prices and recessions.

The Federal Reserve must reinstate the free market to ensure a realistic open-market level of interest rates. This can be done by ensuring that the realistic value of the currency is based upon the value of a metal (gold) that has been used for money for thousands of years. With an accurate value of a basis for the country's currency, the value of goods, assets, and services can be valued reasonably. Gold, like any other substance that is bought and sold in the world, can be reasonably and rationally set by open and free markets. With open and free markets setting the value of the nation's currency, goods, assets, and services can be accepted and traded with confidence. With free and open markets, government statistics such as inflation, GDP, and unemployment will also be reliable for individual and business management decisions.

GOVERNMENT FINANCE PHILOSOPHY THAT WORKS

Use of the Keynesian philosophy has created recurring boom-and-bust cycles in the economy of the United States. With easy funding of government programs, a number of negative results have occurred over the last hundred years. The Keynesian thinking of the Federal Reserve has provided lower-than-normal interest rates that foster oversupply of assets (booms) and the recessions that follow. The consequences that occur along with deflation of asset prices are as follows:

1. Funding for avoidable war or military conflicts, military bases, and activities in other countries unnecessary for the defense of the United States.
2. Funding of government programs that benefit only a select group of citizens that would be more correctly financed and administered by state or local governments.
3. Funding of projects that do not provide a positive return for all citizens, such as pork-barrel projects, to gain votes in key political areas.
4. Funding of programs for the creation, regulation, and staffing of federal bureaucracies that can be better done by state or local governments.
5. Generating a federal program deficit in an operation that does not provide a positive return for the majority of US citizens.
6. Collection of taxes and temporary funding of social security and Medicare programs until those programs' administrative responsibilities can be transferred to states and individuals.

As previously addressed, the effectiveness of the Keynesian philosophy of government has removed the freedom of the individual and replaced it with dependence upon the federal government. As the freedom and responsibility of the individual grows under leadership of moral, honest representatives in a new, commonsense government, a new financing philosophy will grow. A simple, logical means of budgeting and financing government will take hold. Investing in government operations will be based upon return on investment. This means that funds used for an operation, or to purchase or spend on an asset, should give a return equal to or higher than the cost.

Return on investment for an operation means that money or funds used to buy a good or service (a book, training, instructions, use of a tool or a machine, use of a person, or use of your time) should either pay you back in a greater value of money, funds, goods, or services. Notice that time is part of the return math. That means that the amount of time and funds used to perform the operation must be paid back via an equal amount of money or time over the same period.

For example, if you buy a tool for fifty dollars to complete a project using that tool, and are able to complete the project before the tool must be discarded at a zero-dollar value, you have invested fifty dollars to do your project. The investment in the tool to do your project had a return on investment of fifty dollars divided by fifty dollars' worth of tool used on the project, which equals one. If you had not been able to complete the project or operation in less than the time needed, the return on investment in the tool would be less than one, and it would not have been a good return on investment.

Return on investment for an asset or thing of value means that money or funds used to purchase an asset should also either pay you back in a greater value of money or funds over a period of time. For example, if you buy a tool (asset) for fifty dollars and are able to use it for two years to complete your project, before you sell it to someone else for his or her use for ten dollars, you will have a total return on investment of forty dollars divided by ten dollars, equal to four. Dividing four by two years means that you got an average yearly return on investment of 2.0. If you buy all of your tools at a return on investment of 1.0 or higher (than 2.0) you know that you will at least be getting your money's worth on your investment in the asset of tools.

As can be seen by the above examples, public servants need to have a basic understanding of math. It may be a reason why the Keynesian philosophy has been easy for politicians to use. Using this philosophy, the only understanding needed is that the proposed budget number should be higher or larger than an existing or prior budget number. Then a politician only needs to find a reason to appeal to a potential voter that assures him or her that more spending on something is better than past spending. That, of course, means that no analysis or common sense is needed to see if the cause that is being promoted has a good reason to be acted upon. A politician without knowledge of accounting or economics and only a desire for authority is fair game for bad public service. This is very likely the reason why the average businessperson's opinion of Congress and some legislatures is low. With a logical, practical philosophy for budgeting and financing government programs and expenses, citizens' and taxpayers' confidence in their government will return. Using return on investment for budgeting projects or programs will provide that confidence.

GOVERNMENT LEVELS REORGANIZATION

Over the last fifty years, government responsibility and authority have become centered on federal government operations. Managers of state and local governments have had to determine how best to operate to meet federal rules, regulations, and guidelines. Federal regulations provided a one-size-fits-all method of government operation. Local and state conditions and environments were required to fit regulations that sometimes did not apply or make sense where they were enforced. Local and state issues that did not fit federal standards required extra time, funds, and effort to gain rational consideration from federal regulators.

A commonsense reorganization of the various levels of government would start by building the levels of government from the ground up. That means giving the lowest level or local government the highest priority. Higher levels of government could then be built from the level just below them. As mentioned in previous sections, the original government of the United States had only four departments under President Washington. During the first 130 years, the number of departments grew to nine. Of those nine, only six departments would be used today. Of the six, two would likely be used for measurement and limited oversight. With the growth of government and tremendous growth in the debt and deficit, the federal government now has fifteen departments, and many agencies within those departments.

If the levels of government are set up to give individual citizens the highest degree of freedom to reach their greatest potential skills and abilities, then the local government would have the greatest influence. As every person is able to best use their skills, abilities, and resources to his or her advantage, the local government will benefit the most from these activities. It will be the local government's responsibility to use its authority to help the citizens and the economy with the government services that it provides. The local government authority provides order through regulations, local government operations, and government services, and collects sales and property taxes. By guaranteeing the orderly freedom of citizen taxpayers, the local government will help generate business in the local area to grow the economy in the community and the state. By supporting the use of the resources in the local environment, the local government will contribute to growth of the citizens of the community, the state, and the nation.

If the nation is to regain the strength it had at the beginning of the 1900s, it will need to reorganize the levels of government similarly to how they were in that period of time. With a limited federal government that champions the freedom of the individual down to the local level, an effective and efficient operation will be possible. The federal government will be limited to six department heads:

1. Secretary of State
2. Secretary of Defense
3. Secretary of Treasury
4. Attorney General
5. Secretary of the Interior
6. Secretary of Agriculture

The Secretaries of the Interior and Agriculture, like the other national departments, will be limited to measuring and accounting for activities that are administered in each state. The first four of the above departments will be chiefly responsible for managing their operations for the benefit of the United States as a whole, within the country and with respect to relations with other countries. The Departments of Interior and Agriculture will own, operate, and manage federal property in the states, and report major differences between states to help coordinate state activities. Broad federal programs such as social security and Medicare will be operated with the objective of eventually (within twenty years) becoming state-managed and state-operated programs. Until social security and Medicare are transferred to the states, payroll taxes that fund them will be collected along with federal income taxes from payrolls.

With the local governments responsible for providing order for individual citizens and residents in local communities, the state governments will be left responsible for providing order for individuals and local governments within the state. The state will also be responsible for managing and regulating many of the functions and programs now operated by the federal government, outside of the above six national departments. Until tax collections for Social Security and Medicare are delegated to the states, the administration and field operations of those programs will be done by the states. Within each state, the operation and order for state functions will be under the authority of the state. Coordination of operations for individual state citizens and local governments will be under the authority of the state. States will have the right to change or turn down any federal regulation that does not come from the six approved departments of the federal government.

The transition from dominance of the central government to dominance of state and local governments will take time, but it will be liberating. The current operation of all people and resources as though they were all in the same environment will be changed by moving all department and agency functions from Washington to each state. The political influence of Washington lobbyists will be lowered and dispersed among the states. Lobbyists and businesses will need to change their thinking to account for the resources and abilities within each state. The potential for developing local area resources, in relation to the state and other local areas, will focus local and state government where it can best be used. By concentrating the operations of government where it will best serve the country's citizens, the country will achieve effective and efficient government.

BALANCING GOVERNMENT BUDGETS

As previously mentioned with regard to the federal budget, it will be a major challenge to control the growth of federal programs that provide benefits to wide groups of people. It will be necessary to limit the growth of entitlement programs by placing restrictions on how those benefits are paid out. On the national level, it is a challenge to set restriction levels that are appropriate for all geographic regions. For that reason, it will make more sense for each state to administer federal programs until each state takes control of its budget and expenses. Until 2016 or later, when there is a chance for a balanced budget, the existing federal budget programs will continue to increase the national debt with deficit budgets. Balanced budgets will mean that revenues will potentially equal expenses. Expenses will include capital budget principal and interest payments for capital projects financed on twenty-year terms. For capital expenses, there must be at least enough revenue to equal all payments on capital projects, while covering all operating expenses.

Without increasing income taxes, it will be necessary to limit payments for all federal programs by setting standards that will reduce who or what qualifies for payment. By moving payment expenses to levels that are most appropriate for averages within each state, as established by each state individually, payment levels should be reduced. This will replace payment levels set by a national, one-size-fits-all standard. Citizens living in high-cost areas will not get high payment levels as high as those based on state averages. With control over entitlement-program budgets achieved, state administration of programs, and the use of average state payment levels, the growth in cost of benefit programs should be reduced. Reasonable foreign policy activities that limit military police activities to defense of the United States should reduce budget requirements. A program to reduce the national deficit will also reduce interest expenses on the national deficit, even as interest rates rise to normal levels.

Most state and local budgets have been balanced for some time, in all but a few states and local governments. With increased responsibilities in state and local governments and transfer of federal programs to states, there will be higher expenses. The process of transferring federal programs and administration to the states should be less challenging than it may appear. Many state agencies now handle much of the administration of federal programs at the state level. The administrative expenses of the federal government can be transferred to each state based on a prorated expense at the federal level. There will be a cost in time and funds to make the change from federal-level operations of programs to state-level operations. It is obvious that reorganizing from federal-level government operations to state-level operations will not be easy. It will be much better for citizens of state and local governments to have operations that are most appropriate to their area of the country. With government administration and regulations that are mainly geared to local conditions and resources, the effectiveness of those programs will be improved. It is likely that the budget revenues and expenses that are appropriate for each state will be lower for each state than the current total of both national and state budgets.

Benefit programs such as Social Security and Medicare are areas of the budget that will require coordination between federal and state governments. Beginning in 2015 and for twenty years, individuals will have the option of either paying into those programs or participating in savings plans. They can deposit savings for withdrawal for approved expenses such as retirement, income supplements, or medical care. If citizens do not choose to participate in benefits such as Social Security and Medicare, they will have the option of saving up to 10 percent of their pay and deducting it from their income. With savings accounts, people will have control over their own money and can use it as they decide. They will also have the ability to earn as much as they choose to grow their savings, and they can purchase insurance to reduce risk. The savings account also gives the owner the ability to use those funds without restrictions set by a government-regulated program. Those citizens who wish to retain benefit programs such as Social Security and Medicare can continue to pay the higher income tax rate while building savings separately on their own. As more restrictions are placed on government benefit programs, savings deductions from payroll taxes will provide flexibility and control for personal needs. In a country that gives individuals the freedom to make their own choices, all citizens will be able to choose whether to remain in the federal benefit programs or build and manage their own savings.

TAXING FOR GROWTH AND PROGRESS

In addition to fees and charges for services performed by local and state governments, there are really two types of taxes: property and sales taxes. The use of each type of tax will help determine how and for what it will be used. Both types are local taxes and collected at the local government level. With emphasis on freedom of the individual citizen and taxpayer, it is common sense that most of the taxes will be used and spent at the local level. The local government sets the level of taxation for both property and sales taxes. The total taxes collected by the local government depends upon the environment it sets with its regulations, cost of services, utility charges, transportation system, emergency services, education system, and zoning. Most of the expenses of providing services to individual taxpayers are spent at the local level. On that basis, it makes sense that two-thirds of taxes and fees collected at the local level will be spent at that level.

With a majority of local government revenue coming from property and sales taxes, this will mean that most expenses and most activities will occur at the local community level. As a result of most activity by government happening locally, it is likely that most business activity will also occur locally. Use of area resources, with coordination and cooperation of the local government, also impacts other communities and governments in the region. State government has an important role in overseeing business activities in local and regional areas within the state. With oversight, the state is able to measure business activities and ensure that state regulations minimize conflicts and encourage positive business developments. Without the need to be directly involved in local business and government activities, the state will not require the revenue levels that local governments need. With only monitoring of, and coordination with, local governments, the state will not need more than one-third of the revenues that local governments collect from taxes.

State governments receive a high percentage of their revenues from the federal government as a means of implementing federal regulations at the state and local levels. As the majority of federal agencies operations are moved to the states, the same percentage

(37 percent) can continue to go to the state. At the same time, state agencies can continue to carry out federally adopted regulations at the state level, as they have in the past. Federal workers can transfer to the states from federal agencies and be used by the states, as long as they perform state-required operations. State governments can also receive revenues from payments for services that they perform for businesses and individuals needing statewide services. The states can charge for costs incurred in performing services for individuals or businesses, and can charge amounts greater than actual cost. In addition, there are some charges that states can collect for statewide permits that cover all areas within the state, outside of strictly local government charges. Some states may also collect income taxes to make up for some payroll and property taxes collected by local governments. States collecting income taxes appear to place a greater importance on the state taking a dominant role in individual and business activities. With the nation emphasizing freedom of individuals and businesses to reach their potential, it will mean that those states miss growth opportunities.

As can be seen by the previous information provided on taxes, taxation is necessary for the management of individuals so that order can be provided. Without the order that government provides, the world could be ruled by the strongest and most dishonest leaders. With a good government, honest, responsible leaders have an opportunity to govern. Most times, government takes funds from individuals in return for services that government renders. A good government only takes funds (taxes) from people to provide the best service for the least expense necessary.

The federal government funds most of its expenses (approximately 90 percent) with income tax and payroll social insurance taxes. Since most citizens require some services from the federal government, it makes sense that all citizens should contribute toward paying for government.

As can be seen from the description of the tax policies described in Section IV, a minimum tax of 10 percent of income would be required for a citizen who forgoes federal benefits. The same citizen can also deduct up to 10 percent from gross income for keeping a savings account to provide his or her own benefits using his own income.

A citizen who chooses to receive support from federal government benefits will also pay an income tax of 20 percent of gross income, but will not be able to save up to 10 percent of his income in a savings account.

This tax policy provides a fair and equal opportunity for all citizens who work for a living, as proposed by federal government leadership after 2016. This policy also gives individual citizens the freedom to make a choice as to how they contribute to government, how they benefit from government, and how they can use or spend their earnings. With fair and equal free choice allowed for citizens, there can be equal opportunity for all citizens to maximize their potential to benefit from the skills and abilities that God gave them.

In any society there will be times and circumstances where some individuals will need help beyond what a government can provide, or what using their savings requires. As a tax policy, outside of funds in a savings account, an individual should be able to contribute to charitable organizations up to 5 percent of that individual's gross income before the 10 percent or 20 percent mandatory taxes are paid. Helping one's fellow citizens should benefit all free individuals and provide better relations among all people.

REGULATION FOR GROWTH AND PROGRESS

Over the last fifty years, the federal government has become a dominant factor in the economy of the United States. Beginning with social programs in the late 1960s and with the total control of federal government funding, the central government has dominated economic decisions. The strength and vitality of state and regional governments have been lost to regulatory barriers of a one-size-fits-all central government. The obvious benefit of local resource development has been replaced by the many rules and procedures of Washington's central government.

With different resources in virtually every state and locality, it is easy to see how resources can maximize potential in each state and locality. Regulations and procedures set in Washington, with minimal knowledge of local conditions, cannot hope to gain maximum advantage, due to ignorance. The fifteen department members and the agencies under them waste time, effort, and funds with redundant efforts that attempt to treat each state and locality as an average for all fifty states. It is only common sense that at least nine of the fifteen departments can be more effective and efficiently managed and operated in each state.

Each state has different geography, topography, natural resources, transportation resources, education resources, population and society resources, and future prospects. Within each state, localities also have different resources. It is logical and understandable that the people within each locality will use the freedoms granted by the Constitution and Bill of Rights to improve themselves and their economies. With proper local guidance, each locality can maximize its potential. With proper guidance, each state can regulate and coordinate local governments and their activities to maximize the state's potential. State and local governments can best guide, manage, and regulate local resources.

The United States can improve the nation's overall economic performance by moving the regulation and management of each of the federal departments to the states when and where possible. As mentioned in Section IV, the national government would be more efficient and effective if the federal government were limited to six departments. Of the six, two departments (the Departments of Agriculture and the

Interior) could be partially owned and generally overseen at the federal level, but managed at the state level. Those two departments would own property within states, but would have those properties managed by the states in which they were located. This arrangement would be best for maximizing the efficiency and effectiveness of the resources within each state. With each state contributing to positive economic growth and progress, the nation can become the strong, industrial freedom's nation that it was in the past, before it became a centrally controlled debtor country.

The process of reorganizing governments to move operation and management of federal, Washington-based departments to the states will be gradual. As states take over regulatory responsibilities from Washington, it will be the states that determine the human resources needed to ensure efficient and effective government. As much of the actual regulation is carried out by state agencies now, it will be a matter of keeping those rules and procedures that work, while dropping those that do not work. This should be done over a period that will not exceed more than six years to eliminate political difficulties related to members of Congress. Members of Congress from each state would expect that with management and operations focused in their own states, the resulting conflicts between state businesses and federal bureaucracies will be much reduced.

CAPITALISM AND DEMOCRACY CHOICE

By freeing the individual, the government should give each citizen taxpayer a capitalist mind-set. With a capitalist mind-set, each citizen taxpayer will choose what is best for his or her economics. Each citizen is entitled to one vote for government representatives in his or her local area. Unfortunately, this method of voting gives everyone the same choice for who represents them in some level of government. There has been much concern with how those government representatives use the tax dollars that they are given by taxpayers. If all income tax is used by the federal government, it is common sense that those paying the tax should have some impact on how their funds are used. In order to give all citizens a fair choice of who represents them in government, a combination of one vote per citizen, and a voting level based upon income tax paid, makes sense. A change from one vote per citizen to an average of popular votes, and a vote count for income tax paid, would appear to be a just means of representation.

The method of one vote per citizen has a major drawback due to greed and envy. One vote per citizen encourages each voter to vote according to how much the government can be expected to do for him or her. With those making higher levels of income paying for the majority of government expenses, the voter is guided to vote for more benefits at the expense of those making a higher income. This is a government level of enforced charity that forces higher-income citizens to provide benefits to lower-income citizens. This eliminates the free will of all citizens. Lower-income citizens are provided benefits that they would have not earned by choosing what will best support themselves and their family. Those citizens are thus no better than slaves to government dependence, without the joy and satisfaction of any achievement. With little or no achievement to show for it, the dependent citizen will lack the pride of a full life.

The high-income, high achievement citizen is forced to reduce his or her standard of living by paying higher levels of taxes to improve the use of his or her resources (time, labor, and abilities). Thus the high-achievement citizens are discouraged from working harder to gain higher pay and income by taking even less home for themselves and their families. It is common sense to have a voting system that gives all voters an equal say in how government uses their tax dollars.

LEGAL SYSTEMS FOR ORDER AND PROGRESS

The ultimate sources of order in the United States are the Constitution and Bill of Rights. The Supreme Court of the United States is the final interpreter of federal constitutional law. It also has ultimate appellate jurisdiction over federal courts and state court cases involving federal law. The makeup of the court, and the outcomes of its cases, vary according to the source of their nomination by the president and confirmation by the Senate. Depending upon what political party has gained control over the nominating process, the decisions can be considered more conservative (leaning toward strict interpretation of the Constitution) or liberal (leaning toward wider interpretation or activist interpretation of the Constitution). Although adequate ability to enforce original wording in the Constitution and amendments exists, broad interpretations have created many confusing and misleading details to regulations in the federal bureaucracy.

The founding fathers' intent with the Constitution and Bill of Rights was to give the individual the freedom of choice with regard to religion, business dealings, and government. Over the history of Supreme Court decisions there has been a trend of giving central government more power, while giving state governments, local governments, and individuals less power. This has occurred with political leaders who favored more power for government control. The Federal Reserve has made it easier for elite members of political parties and the financial community to gain power by providing improved, so-called benefits to citizens in exchange for votes. Citizens were encouraged to vote for politicians by exchanging morality and honesty for selfish benefits. Voting by choosing what one thinks is best is in keeping with the intent of the founding fathers with regard to individual freedom. Voting like that, however, betrays the ability of individuals to use common sense to choose what is best in the long run for themselves and their families.

With the Federal Reserve gaining congressional support by helping congresspersons to get elected, it has become the strongest arm of government, especially since gold was dropped as the basis for money. The partnership between the Federal Reserve and Congress has created a dishonest and immoral democracy. It will take honest, responsible, moral leaders to change the direction of the government and the United States. Though possible, it may take severe and drastic circumstances for citizens to elect the type of leaders who can bring about the change. With the right type of leaders from out of the public, the president and political party leaders will build a Supreme Court that will follow the intent of our nation's founders in making their decisions.

The Supreme Court not only guides by appeals but also sets an example for state and local courts. With new leadership in all areas of government, fair and just order can be obtained so that the nation can progress and become the Freedom's Nation that it once was.

WHAT YOU CAN DEPEND UPON

Individual citizens and residents now depend upon the government and its directives to determine when, where, and how to act. This has been a mistake, as many have seen in their private lives. The guidelines that the founders of this country gave us have long been forgotten or revised. The founders relied upon God, as evidenced by the mention of God in many founders' communications. God gave humans a soul, as Jesus Christ provided us with an example. If each human must depend upon someone or something else for guidance in his or her life, it should be God and not the government. God gave us the Ten Commandments to guide us in how to live. By following those guidelines, the soul of each human has the opportunity to live a good life and join God in heaven. The opportunity for reward after a good life is diminished only by the faults of human choices in one's life.

The opportunity for success in the world is also dependent upon the choices you make in your life. If you follow Christian guidelines as well as those given by the Constitution and Bill of Rights while maximizing the abilities that God gave you, you can be successful. As a citizen, it is up to you to use the freedom that God gave you to make the most of your life and your abilities to gain the happiness that is your right.

Conclusion - Freedom's Nation in Practice by 2030

INDIVIDUAL FREEDOM OF CHOICE

The direction and leadership of the country must be changed to focus on increasing the power and authority of the individual within the operations of federal, state, or local governments. In recent years, the growth of the authority and power of the federal government increased until numerous scandals slowly destroyed public faith in it. At the same time, growth in the US federal budget deficit slowly reduced the faith and support of nations that trade with and financially support the nation. Elections in 2014 and 2016 identified alternative public thinking that magnified the need for regaining the belief in freedom of choice for the individual. Knowledge of the history of the Colonial Revolution and the Constitution and Bill of Rights was revived. With that knowledge, the US public supported new national leaders who believed in the strength of individual freedom. The new nation's leaders then produced new federal legislation that gave authority back to the individual citizen. Each individual citizen will now have the right to make his or her own choices within the legal jurisdiction of federal, state, or local governments. Every person will have the right to choose how he or she lives as long as they do not physically or financially harm others.

Public Activity: Each person will live according to the laws and regulations within the local and state jurisdiction where he or she resides. The activity of each person that does not cause harm to another person or group is judged as private and respected by others, including the government. If a person has committed no crime, or is not suspected of committing a crime, no branch of government has the right to view or record communications or actions by that person.

Where one resides is up to the individual, depending upon his or her choice of work or career, local environment, skills or abilities, personal resources, and religious preference. The existence of a supreme being is accepted. References to Christian beliefs and religious texts are accepted but not prevented by law. Prayers are allowed, but not required, at public gatherings and meetings as long as they are nondenominational. Discrimination is illegal when and if it causes harm to individuals or groups. State and local governments can place limitations or restrictions on individuals or groups, if the majority of the public in that jurisdiction determines so by a vote. There is no minimum required wage level. Choices of where to work, and payment for that work, are per agreement between the individual and his or her employer.

Education: Standards for education will not be set at the national level. Education standards will be set by each state government and administered by school districts within each state. Education of children through high school will be provided by locally funded school districts from local property taxes. The children will be able to choose the school to which each child's school tax allocation is given, based on the cost of educating each child in the local school district.

The school district is governed by elected board members from within the district. Education standards for school districts within a state are modified by the school district board to meet standards appropriate for the area served by the school district. College- and university-level education is set by each educational institution and is funded by that institution with funds from those attending. State funds for advanced educational institutions are limited to the cost of educating each student with state taxes or fees from the state budget. Those state funds are allocated to colleges within the state based upon the appropriate business activity nearest the college.

Outside of limited state funds, those institutions must develop their own sources of income and funding to support the advanced education of each student. Each advanced educational institution will have its own governing board, elected by the alumni of that institution.

Because education and learning are key components of the abilities of individuals in their working lives, they are also necessary to growth in the economy of local areas. If individuals can improve their own economics and the economics of their employers, the result will be growth in personal and business incomes. With each local school system educating its students to suit business activities in the local area, both the individual student and local businesses will benefit. As the local businesses improve, they will expand their income and their hiring. With local businesses growing and improving their economics, the state's finances will improve. As each state's economy improves, so will the nation's economy. As the nation's economy improves and the national GDP improves, there will be more opportunities for workers, and there will be lower unemployment. With the nation's education providing improved opportunities for individuals, economic growth can help make "Freedom's Nation" a vibrant industrial country again.

Laws and Regulations: Most of the federal government's operations will be administered by the six cabinet divisions, with the exception of the Departments of the Interior and Agriculture. Those two departments will only operate and administer the properties owned by the federal government. The Departments of State, Treasury, and Defense, as well as the Attorney General, will operate and administer national issues and handle appeals from state and local governments on undecided issues. The other eleven divisions of the 2013 federal government will be operated and administered by the state governments. By managing those operations from states, where regional and local conditions are better known, both effectiveness and efficiency will be realized. Time and effort for each function will be reduced because management decisions can be made closer to home, and the necessary creation and transfer of federal paperwork can be eliminated.

Freedom of the individual to make choices will not only help the individual but also give state and local government officials the responsibility to make efficient and effective decisions. Efficient and effective decisions made by government officials most familiar with the conditions involved in the decision process will improve the one-size-fits-all process of federal officials in Washington. With more decisions made at state and local levels close to the sources of the issues, the ability of government, and US citizens' confidence in that ability, will be improved.

With more rules and regulations administered from the state and local levels, there will be opportunities for state and local government to set rules and laws. With local and regional conditions considered, it is more likely that some commonsense laws can be introduced.

Commonsense thinking will be more appropriate than maintaining central control of the entire nation to solve a one-in-a-million problem.

One of the nation's major problems is the enforcement of laws for victimless crimes. Individuals should be free to make choices to be compliant with the law in accord with individual freedom of choice. They should be limited to charges or punishments for causing physical or financial harm to other individuals or groups. Limiting punishment to victimless crimes will reduce government costs associated with resources needed to house people in prisons. Broader interpretation of victimless crimes will encourage changes to drug laws. Changes to those laws will further change laws relating to taxes for drugs. Those taxes will be used to educate children about the harm that some drugs can do to the human body and mind. With education that encourages avoiding harmful drugs, young people will reduce the market for drugs that are now considered illegal. Law enforcement will spend less time and funds on enforcing and imprisoning people for drug law violations. The taxes from drug sales will pay for education to avoid drug problems, and will pay for rehabilitation of those who are addicted to the most harmful drugs. Limiting punishment for crimes other than those causing physical or financial harm to others will reduce government expenses for enforcing and punishing people for crimes in general. With demand for illegal drugs reduced, taxes on sales, and taxes on income from sales, will be lower but will not be eliminated. Victimless crimes will reduce the number of criminal activities that are related to drugs. Those activities will include auto accidents, robberies, prostitution, and conflicts between rival drug organizations. Law enforcement can concentrate on ensuring the payment of drug sales taxes and income from the sale of drugs. The safety of individuals and the general public would be improved, and the cost of law enforcement would be reduced.

By moving operation and management of many of the present federal government departments to the states, effective and efficient government operations can be attained. Not only will government operations improve how law enforcement works, but also confidence in its ability will be raised. Freedom's nation will give its citizens the security of a well-run government—one that had been lost over the last few years.

BUSINESS AND MARKETS

The depression that started in 2007 and hit its bottom in 2009 was the result of congressional regulation that made it easier to purchase real estate with little or no adequate income. It was further aided by the Federal Reserve's keeping interest rates lower than commonsense finance operation would choose to avoid a housing price boom. This was the common practice for the Fed to reduce risk to the public by accommodating Congress to gain votes with increased benefits for the public. As has been the case in the Fed's history, reducing risks for the public increases the possibility for an overspending boom. As in the 1920s and 1930s, an over exuberant boom (the Roaring Twenties) led to a hard, very deep bust (the Great Depression).

As the Fed did in the 1930s, increasing support for congressional spending with higher levels of federal-level project funding, so it has done since 2008. That Federal Reserve policy of high levels of Fed funding with more dollars has failed in its attempt to increase economic activity and reduce unemployment. Easier access to money did help the US economy in the late 1930s and through World War II by supporting the risk of increased industrial production to gear up for a major military conflict. Reducing risk since 2008 has reduced incentives for business and industry, with nothing gained by taking risks of increased production and the increased hiring of people. Legislation by Congress will reorganize the Federal Reserve so that it will be led by business leaders instead of elite bankers and finance board members. Business leaders will understand the risk-reward basis of managing business and industrial operations. Banker financial leaders do not understand how to take risks because they do not manage operations that directly impact the public. They manage other people's money, not their own.

The Federal Reserve will be audited to identify what should have been done to recover from the 2007–2009 depression. New leadership in Congress and of the nation will then reorganize the Federal Reserve board to include business and industry leaders as staff. With board members focused on business improvement for the nation, a realistic market-oriented basis for valuing the US dollar will be identified. Because gold has been the historic means of valuing a currency, it will become the basis for valuing the currency of the United States. The value of the currency used in exchange for goods and services will be determined by the conversion of a dollar to a quantity of gold. Gold will be the basis for all US dollar transactions.

The nation's economy will be guided by the Treasury, with a division called the Federal Reserve managing the funding of federal government expenditures. The Federal Reserve manages the interest rates on expenses that Congress authorizes to spend on federal operations. The interest rates and volume of federal Treasury bonds will be based upon the federal budget level that the Secretary of the Treasury and the Federal Reserve Board approve.

The Federal Reserve will be composed of twelve regional business leaders nominated by regional state governors and approved by Senate and House congress people from that region. The federal budget will be balanced with operating and capital expenses, covering each year's operating expenses and paying off all capital expense projects with principal and interest based upon twenty-year terms. A 5 percent fund from the budgeted expenses total will be set aside for spending for emergencies such as hurricanes, earthquakes, and floods. Emergency funds not used in a particular year will be carried into the next year's budget.

Interest rates on federal securities will be managed by the Federal Reserve and set by the international market, as opposed to the Federal Reserve creating dollars to buy bonds. The rates will be based upon confidence in funding US federal expenses and the ability to receive payments on the bonds. With a deficit-reduction plan in effect and annual decreases in the total deficit, confidence in bond payments will minimize the interest cost of the bonds. With interest rates providing realistic cost of capital and money that has a real value, economic activity can increase.

Economic decisions can be made without an overabundance of worthless currency. With the Federal Reserve monitoring federal budget growth, instead of an endless amount of funds, Congress will generate balanced budgets to ensure low, realistic interest rates. Realistic interest rates that banks will pay on savings will provide funds for business loans. Risk will be reintroduced into the operation of the nation's economy. The nation's banks, led by a business-oriented Federal Reserve, will work for the benefit of business and not for the large banks and the elite financial leaders. With gold-backed currency, consumers will have realistic prices for goods and services. The nation's businesses will grow as consumers increase spending concurrent with expanding employment.

GOVERNMENT BUDGETS AND FINANCE

With oversight of the congressional budget by the Treasury and Federal Reserve, the annual increase in the nation's federal budget will be limited to an acceptable level for economic growth. As outlined above, the growth of the federal budget will be orderly and will follow commonsense thinking. Changes made to the management of the federal budget deficit will be underway for it to be eliminated within thirty years. Confidence of the public and international trading nations will be improved. The US currency will be recognized as the international reserve currency used for transactions between countries.

Balanced budgets will keep the federal budget from growing at the high rate that has been the practice in past years. One budget area that has been a concern with past budgets has been the growth of entitlements that exceed the growth of tax revenues. Entitlement spending has been reduced as restrictions and limitations were introduced in the early years of new national leadership, per previously mentioned policies.

As entitlement spending now exists, it is handled within each state, which will use knowledge of local conditions to allocate it appropriately using common sense. Federal and state welfare spending will be limited to only a few specific instances where individual savings programs do not provide sufficient funding. Federal revenue will balance with federal welfare spending done at the state level, as all wage earners will pay a federal income tax, depending upon whether they choose to belong to the federal entitlement program. At a minimum, all wage earners will pay an income tax of at least 10 percent. With the 10 percent option, individual wage earners will be able to save up to 10 percent of their gross income in a savings account (free of tax) that they manage themselves, instead of taking entitlements. See simple growth-supporting tax policies in Section IV.

Beyond limiting entitlement programs such as Social Security and Medicare to a set standard benefit level according to time and contribution (via taxes or fees), there will need to be limits set on maximum benefit payments. Benefit payment levels will be set to ensure that all participants in the entitlement option of the federally approved benefits program receive some aid. To ensure a continuing benefit for all participants who have become fully vested for a maximum benefit level, there must be a limit to benefits paid to those who are not fully vested. Therefore aid for nonstandard crisis situations must be limited to a time and an amount, or tax and fee levels will need to be increased for all participants.

When individual savings plans and general tax and fee levels are unable to provide a person sufficient funds or time to address a situation, certain limits will be required. As an example, a limit of six months of continuing income would be set for an individual who had participated in at least a year of the entitlement program option. An additional month of income could be added for each additional year that the individual participated in the program. The total amount of income for payment will be based upon the level of pay the person receives while working. The program as described will limit the growth that the federal budget will add for entitlements over the years.

Balancing the federal budget will require more than bringing entitlements under control. In general, it will take a different method of managing all expenses—both capital and operating expenses that contribute to the budget. As previously mentioned, a management tactic for controlling and organizing expenses is the tactic of return on investment. This means that government operations must use the same common sense that many do in managing their personal finances. Those government operations must ensure that funds invested in a capital project or an operation deliver at least a return equal to, or higher than, the expense. Capital projects must deliver an equal or better return over the life of the capital investment. Operating expenses must deliver an equal or better return over the time required to complete the operational task.

By setting a return level for capital or operating expenses, the total expense can thus be controlled using common sense. For a particular government operation, the top management levels must exhibit strong leadership to set reasonable return levels. Where budget control allows deficits to grow beyond revenue levels, major management-level changes are necessary.

As previously mentioned when I was discussing reorganizing the levels of government, a strategy of moving the administration of federal programs to the states and local government for regulation and operation will have a positive effect. Replacing the one-size-fits-all federal government administration of programs allows operation of them by areas that are knowledgeable of and familiar with local resources (labor issues, geographic descriptions, social issues, business interests, transportation issues, and resource surplus and deficiency items).

By shifting operations management to closer, more familiar locations, the programs will not only reduce the number of people involved, but will also make their operations more effective and efficient and better accepted. Not as much time is used in moving information to and from state and local government operations to federal operations, and the number of people involved at the different government levels is minimized. This thought process is in keeping with focusing government on freedom of the individual. By doing that, satisfying the individual within the local government jurisdiction will better ensure that they will be pleased with how the programs are operated. With the focus on individual freedom of choice, government at all levels—but particularly at the lower levels—will take the responsibility for providing the best service for the least expense.

DEFENSE FOCUSED MILITARY AND INTERNATIONAL BUDGET

At least 20 percent of the national budget has been in the military and foreign affairs sections. The US has been involved for over twenty years in Middle East military actions. It also has military bases in approximately 120 countries. Although a military presence may be needed in some countries to protect US citizens and industries in those countries, it is unlikely that the investment in those military operations protects or defends US territory. In 2012, the United States ranked number one in military spending of all countries. Of the top six countries—the United States, China, Russia, United Kingdom, Japan, and France—the United States spends more than two-and-a-half times as much as China and Russia combined. The US share is 39 percent of the world's total military expenditures by major countries.

Many bases around the world may be for protection of allied countries in Europe, Asia, or the Americas. With the United States spending such a high percentage of world military funds (39 percent), and China and Russia spending less than 15 percent of the world's military funds, this seems excessive. The military spending by the United States is 4.4 percent of its GDP, while the average of all nations' spending is only 2.5 percent. Considering the GDP of the United States is better than twice the GDP of China (which is in second place), this looks even more excessive. With all of the above statistics considered, and with new leadership from 2016 onward, it would only make good sense for the country to reduce spending for military and foreign affairs by 2030.

With strong, responsible leadership to gain control of the federal budget, military spending will have to be reduced. In order to cut back without reducing the security of the nation, a program of national defense must decrease its spending gradually. The United States cannot be depended on to defend countries and causes that should rightfully be able to defend themselves. This will mean that some countries will need to make use of their own militaries for their countries' defenses, and not expect the United States to subsidize their defense.

The United States must use its economic and trade strength to support countries that benefit the citizens and industries within this country. The leadership of the United States will make it clear to the other countries that it will direct efforts to stronger defense of its territories, and will use trade with others to support the US value of freedom. No military action will be taken against a nation except in the defense of another nation, and only with the authorization of Congress. Military bases in allied countries or in US territories can be sold or traded to reduce the US budget over at least a six- to eight-year period.

At the same time, military bases in US territories will be upgraded with the highest level of technological equipment, people, and facilities. This gradual strategy will reduce the military budget to no more than 3 percent of the US GDP. The number of military personnel will be reduced as military bases are eliminated. Military personnel, at the onset of reductions, will be trained to move into civilian jobs where civilian positions are in short supply. Military equipment such as planes, tanks, missiles, and various armaments will be sold to allies to supply their own defense. Military equipment and personnel will not be sold or given to any nations that exhibit offensive threats or actions against allied nations.

With a new strategic military direction, relations with other countries will be improved. The jealousy of less economically active countries will be reduced. Nations and organizations with strong desires for power over others will dislike the freedom supported by the United States. By reducing the authority and responsibility of the United States to interfere in other nations' activities, many nations will shift their own politics to a similar view of individual freedom. The United States can slowly become a model that will encourage other nations to become like "Freedom's Nation."

TRADE FOR ECONOMIC GROWTH, REVENUE, AND EMPLOYMENT

The United States was a powerful industrial nation in the 1950s that spent its wealth on conflicts or wars (those are different words for the same thing), and transitioned to a debt-laden consumer nation. This happened because of shortsighted, ignorant US political leaders who used ready, easy funding by the Federal Reserve to weaken its economy and confidence in its leadership. Politicians who desired government offices used readily available funding from the Federal Reserve to buy votes with promises of favors from government. The same politicians neglected to consider the long-term benefits and needs of voting citizens. The immediate desires of citizens were only considered to gain their votes.

Without the oversight of the management of the economy actually considering what was really needed by the citizens, politicians simply proposed what was immediately needed to get votes. With no rational consideration of the long-term economics of the nation, it became easier to believe in an economic philosophy that placed no limit on benefitting voters. With politicians thinking that there was no limit on spending, it was easier to increase citizens' benefits to gain their votes. When, in 1971, a beleaguered president dropped gold from support of the nation's currency, the Federal Reserve was given the opportunity to fund government spending without using the nation's gold reserves to back the currency. This allowed the Federal Reserve and the Treasury to fund government spending with a currency that could simply be printed without limit.

From 1971 until today, the federal government has funded many extensions to the budget and has generated increases to the national debt. **The projected budget for 2015 is nearing seventeen trillion dollars. It was only around one trillion dollars in 1971. This nation's debt, from totals generated by derivative losses in the 2008 depression, is estimated to be over two hundred trillion dollars.**

The nation's economy is at its lowest point in its entire history because of the ambitions of ignorant politicians and the poor management of the country's economy by the Federal Reserve. The Federal

Reserve's philosophy of unlimited funding of spending has used the excuse of avoiding deflation to fight the last war of the Great Depression. This has been used by politicians to sell the public on the need to create more currency in the hope of generating more economic activity by providing an unlimited amount of money. All this has done is funnel money to the large financial companies, which built up many trillions of debt during the 2008 depression on bad loans on real estate.

The current federal government's hope is that, somehow, economic activity generated by spending printed money will increase growth and eventually pay off the nation's debt and enormous deficit. Most citizens, still hurting from the loss of work and decreased income since 2008, are victims as the country just sinks deeper in debt. Millions of citizens are unemployed or employed far below their potential. The country's leadership wants to keep all citizens at a mediocre existence level of socialist operation, to keep them under control and dependent. The people of this country have gone from freeing slaves in the 1860s to becoming slaves in the 2010s.

The nation is in need of reverting back to what made it a great power during the first 150 years of its existence. That means that the United States must become a great trading nation. To become a great trading nation, the governments of the country must support business and industry that makes products less expensively and of better quality. As God gave the original colonies great natural resources to build their strength, the nation is being given a second chance to use its current resources to build a better country. The energy industry that helped drive the country's industry of the 1800s can now lead the country back to a level of prominence. God has helped develop a new technology that allows an abundant and inexpensive source of oil and gas to be produced from below the surface of the land. That technology is called "fracking", which allows energy companies to recover oil and gas from geologic stone formations. Those companies drill vertically, then horizontally to extend pipe through shale formations. After extending through the formations, the pipe is fractured and high pressure water and sand are injected into the shale formation. This process frees oil and gas to flow through the pipe to the surface for various energy uses.

With low-cost energy and a government that supports the God-given right of individual freedom, the business and industry of the country can be revived. This revival can happen if the leadership of the federal, state, and local governments supports freedom of the individual so that no harm to others is permitted. With this type of leadership, the nation can move forward to an improved economy. After more than forty-five years of concentrated power in a central government, it will require some revolutionary changes in the citizens' thinking. If the people running for office promote individual freedom and all of the positive results possible, those revolutionary changes can become reality. As the revolution in thought takes hold, the economies of people, towns, counties, states, and finally the country will improve.

As improvement takes place from the people to towns, counties, states, and the nation, trade with other businesses in towns, counties, states, and nations will grow. Trade between different entities helps both sides by supplying needed shortages in return for improving the revenue of the supplier. This is no less than capitalism at work. Capitalism and business have been considered by socialist believers to be negative types of operation because they actually improve both sides of a transaction. Socialist thinking only takes away from a business activity because one side gives up wealth, and the other side gives up freedom. God gave individuals freedom to improve themselves, and never meant for it to be taken away.

Growing trade among the people and businesses will gradually improve the economy of individuals and the businesses of which they are a part. Growth of trade in the economies of the various levels of government will improve the influence of those governments. That influence will grow stronger with governments and businesses in other nations. This will mean that relations with other nations and their businesses will grow stronger as help and improvements are delivered with trade transactions. The power of the US governments will increase with trade with other countries.

As the power of the various levels of government increases, the greatest increase will be in the negotiating power of the federal government. If the freedom of the individual can be maintained by the levels of government, the United States will have an improved economy and will have the ability to influence the economies and politics of other nations. Instead of using military force to influence change in other countries, the United States will have the force of trade. Thus through trade, the United States will not only have the ability to help other countries but will also be able to lead other countries with positive actions. Freedom's Nation can once again become a leader in international affairs.

As the country uses the benefit of ample low-cost energy and the desire of individuals to improve their lives, opportunities for employment will follow. There will be a major growth of jobs in the energy fields of exploration, production, production treatment, pipeline construction, refining, and distribution system operation, as well as manufacture of energy-related products. The low-cost energy used for transportation as well as products made with hydrocarbons will transform the United States into a strong competitor for industrial goods in the world. Jobs will not only grow in the field of energy production, but energy will also generate jobs downstream from the production.

The energy technology of horizontal drilling, coupled with high-pressure injection of water, sand, and detergents ("fracking"), was started in the United States. It is still early in developing the oil and gas resources available. Because of its early development in the United States, coupled with highly developed oil- and gas-processing technology, the United States is far ahead of other countries. Even though labor rates for people in the United States are higher than in many other countries, this country will be able to produce energy more cheaply than other countries. This should create an abundance of opportunities for citizens in a free competitive market. Over the next five years, the US unemployment rate should gradually drop.

For individuals who are willing to work hard, there will be jobs available in energy-related fields. Those jobs in the energy fields often will pay above-normal wages because some of the tasks require risk of injury. All that is keeping the unemployment rate from falling across the country is regulation by the federal government. With federal and state governments freeing the labor and energy markets to allow commonsense regulation, the energy industry will power an improved employment picture for Freedom's Nation.

Energy is the one factor that is a major part of every country's cost of living. It not only impacts the cost of living for individuals in each country, but it also impacts the cost of the industrial goods of each country. Today the United States has a major advantage in its cost of energy over major industrial producers of goods such as Europe and China. Those countries pay a multiple of the United States' cost per million energy units. In some cases, it is double or triple the cost. With limited technology development in those areas, the United States has an even greater advantage in cost of delivered goods.

The loss of labor competition from the 2008 depression has kept increases in labor rates low enough to keep energy production and processing costs in the United States competitive. The low cost of energy in the United States gives the industrial products of this country an advantage in competition. This advantage can make industrial products from the United States a major choice for supplies for businesses in other nations. With minimum common-sense labor and benefit regulations in the United States, there is no reason why this country can't again become the leading industrial nation in the world. This will take time and a federal government that places more importance on being competitive in the industrial marketplace. With leadership from Congress and reorganization of the Federal Reserve, more importance can be placed on industrial and financial competitiveness. With leadership of the nation improved to favor freedom of the individual, and by allowing states and local governments to manage local economies, Freedom's Nation can again become the leading industrial country in the world.

As unemployment is reduced and business increases locally and internationally, incomes will grow. With incomes growing for individuals, businesses, and industries, the total revenue from the federal income tax will increase. This is the objective that the Keynesian Federal Reserve was trying to obtain. However, using printed dollars to help large financial institutions simply pay off debts for derivative losses has not improved energy production. Improved energy production is helping the people of this country produce more revenue with their efforts. With changes in how the government is run, incentives from personal improvements obtained through freedom of choice will improve each individual's economics. As individuals improve their economics, they contribute to the economics of their businesses. As every business improves, they contribute to the economics of their government. With individuals, businesses, and governments improving their economics, the nation will gain improved economics.

The strategy of the United States becoming a trading nation will produce the following results:

1. Greater opportunity for employment and low unemployment.
2. Leading the world by making competitive industrial products.
3. Increased government revenues from more trading activity.

In the end, the strategy of becoming a trading nation will help the country regain the title of the leading industrial nation in the world. Freedom's Nation will then become the world's leading industrial nation, as well as the world's leading nation.

FREEDOM'S NATION FOR US CITIZENS

The goal of reducing risk for all citizens and for all activities has been replaced. Instead of blaming some other person, group, or organization for negative events in our lives, we now have some control and some choice. We can feel safe and secure in a country that places more emphasis on providing the opportunity to improve our lives than restricting them in some way to improve all others' lives.

Work is encouraged to gain better education and job opportunities. During our educational years, we have freedom as to what school we attend with education funds in a local area school system. A school can be chosen that provides the type of education that best suits training for the type of work that we may want to do. The schools in each area of a state will educate and train their students for the type of businesses or industries in the local area. While in school and when in higher education, we will be able to work for a business or industry that will pay us based upon the quantity and quality of our work. Pay will be based upon our efforts at the level of what we and our supervisor determine is fair, instead of by a government agency.

As we complete our education and training for a job, we will feel happy that there are jobs available and that the businesses that offer work are flexible in their ability to provide benefits for us. If we become better at our work, we will feel satisfied that we and our employers can determine pay and benefits that feel fair to all of us. If we have the opportunity for a better-paying position with better benefits, we know that there are other choices out there because the country's economy is strong.

When employed in a job, we can choose either to pay a maximum income tax of 20 percent, so that we can use retirement and medical benefits provided by the government; or we can choose to pay a reduced income tax of only 10 percent so that we can save up to 10 percent of our pay in a personal savings account that we manage ourselves. Our personal savings accounts can be used to supplement company-sponsored retirement accounts as well as provide medical benefits funds in retirement years. We appreciate freedom of choice with regard to whether we take a government benefit option and with regard to how we manage our personal savings accounts with that option.

As for pay and the amount of taxes that we pay, the choices that we have for government benefits or personal savings allow us to manage our costs of living within our abilities. We feel good about having choices as to how we can manage our life with regard to obligations to the government and the ability to manage our personal finances.

We are able to work in a country with a currency that has a basis of reality in gold, which has been used for money for centuries. The value of goods and services can be related to something that has been used to buy and sell items throughout history. Government data that tells us what our requirements are for our daily lives is realistic and understandable because we can see whether the cost of things went up or down in our lives. There is no need for the Treasury or government leaders to adjust the numbers to support the latest objective that the state has decided on. Honesty has become a common trait among the leaders of Congress and the presidency. Whether conditions change for the good or bad, we can depend upon our leaders to tell us the truth. We can have faith in the money that we use, and faith in a government that is able to honestly provide it for us. The direction of the economy is under the control of government leaders who address the public's needs through the action of our government's congressional representatives.

The economy is managed by a combination of the Treasury and the Federal Reserve Board. The Secretary of the Treasury is chosen by the president and approved by both houses of Congress. The Federal Reserve Board is composed of members nominated by the governors of the twelve regions of the United States and approved by both houses of Congress. With the Federal Reserve Board members chosen from prominent, successful business leaders and overseen by Congress, the citizens will know that their desires are fully considered. The direction of the nation's economy will then be moving toward the direction of the collective desires of all citizens. The general direction of the nation's economy will see a gradual improvement, as one would expect of only a small percentage of growth each year. That small percentage of growth will be limited by keeping the standard of living conditions to a reasonable increase or decrease to avoid extreme changes in prices for goods and services. The drastic booms and busts of economic activity are avoided.

Stability of the economy is an objective of a good Federal Reserve. With the public directly choosing who manages the economy, there will no one to blame for problems with the economy other than the citizens themselves. It is up to each citizen to function within the economy to make the most progress that his or her abilities allow.

With the Federal Reserve Board and the Treasury overseeing the budget, there will be balanced budgets from Congress that include paying down the federal deficit in thirty years. The balanced budgets will not include growth in entitlement spending to inflate the budgets in future years. The growth will be limited because those receiving the benefits will be required to be vested for a set number of years to gain full payments. Foreign buyers of US bonds will feel confident in the country's ability to pay off the bonds as they mature. This will lower interest rates that international buyers of US debts will have to pay, and thus keep the federal deficit from growing at an increasingly large rate. Citizens who buy US bonds will be paid a competitive rate and will also be able to get higher rates on savings at banks. With higher savings amounts available, banks will be able to make profitable loans available for US businesses. With loans available at reasonable rates, businesses can grow in accordance with markets for their products.

With the Federal Reserve operating within a free market and with balanced budgets, interest rates will be set by the international bond market. The interest rate on US bonds will be set by a free market, rather than set by Fed purchases of bonds with printed money. The market for US bonds will be managed by a Federal Reserve that will now be part of Freedom's Nation.

The US dollar has now regained the title of "world's reserve currency," after doubts about its ability because of the growth and size of the country's federal deficit. Major reserve growth of dollars in other countries that are major US bond purchasers had declined. Trade agreements between China and many large, financially stable countries had increased the use of the Chinese currency or *yuan*, instead of the dollar. With lower reserve growth of dollars in bond-purchasing countries, there was concern that the dollar would lose the "world reserve currency" title. It was possible for the United States to regain reserve currency status by the following accomplishments:

1. Audit of the Federal Reserve.
2. Reorganizing the Federal Reserve.
3. Stopping the growth of the US federal deficit with control of federal spending.
4. Balancing budgets in the future for the United States.
5. Planning a reduction and elimination of the federal budget deficit.
6. Reducing foreign military activity and increasing trade with other nations.

There is now a plan to eliminate in thirty years the federal deficit, which had become impossible to address for a number of years. The growth in the federal budget that had been propelling the deficit higher has been reduced with balanced budgets. The areas of the federal budget that had been contributing to its growth with entitlements and military spending have been brought under control with common sense and limited return on investments. Federal assets within the country, such as the Postal Service and Tennessee Valley Authority, will be sold, as will other assets that can be managed just as well by corporations.

By coming to grips with the federal debt and bringing it under control, the federal government can follow an example that has been used by many states and local governments. Some states and local governments operate with balanced budgets that do not build deficits over long periods of time. Individual citizens can be satisfied that the government of all is able to manage its finances, as many of them have had to all their lives. Citizens can take pride in witnessing the ability of the country to reduce the pressure of carrying an enormous and growing deficit. The ability of private individuals to invest in government bonds with confidence will be revived. As the confidence of individual citizens grows, so will the confidence of financially strong countries that buy US bonds. The nation's ability to finance its expenses will become improved with reasonable interest rates and ready bids of all terms of bonds.

The average citizen can feel secure that the economy of his or her country is stable and growing. Improvements to the government provide opportunities in the nation's economy. There is less stress from the possibility of military conflicts that may change the environment of the area of the country in which a citizen lives. Whether to serve in the military to serve one's country is a choice that one is free to make. The possibility of military conflicts in countries supplying fuel, energy, food, or other aspects necessary for living standards has been reduced by a strategy to use trade instead of military force to influence other countries. Changes in the cost of living from international trade are minimized by a strong and active government in both foreign and domestic dealings.

The role of the government has been changed from reducing risk to individuals, to reducing risk from government. The freedom that has been given to individuals has allowed each person to reduce his or her own risks by acting responsible for himself or herself and avoiding harm to others. The new role of government is one of providing the freedom to individuals that gives them the opportunity to maximize their abilities and talents.

The role for each individual citizen is to be an independent, responsible person. The success of each person will be dependent upon how well he or she works with other citizens. All citizens support their country in its relations with other countries. Trade with businesses and individuals from other countries is carried on in a fair and responsible manner. US conflicts with other countries are avoided by using trade relationships before resorting to military actions. If conflicts with other countries require military action, those actions will be supported financially only as long as it takes to protect US citizens or US businesses from immediate harm.

US citizens can feel secure that their country has faith in individuals to make their own choices regarding how they live their lives. Each person is given the freedom and support that was guaranteed by the founders of the country. The government expects each citizen to act independently and responsibly. Citizens' relationships respect others' freedom and independence. Businesses and companies that hire people are respected for their efforts and the right to earn a living or make a profit. Businesses and companies are given the same respect that citizens are expected to give one another. Individuals support the governments in the region or area of the country in which they live, and support government actions that encourage and assist business. Individuals know that government can be a help or a hindrance to a business, and support actions by governments that are positive for business.

Citizens of the United States can feel secure that they will have the freedom to take risks themselves to improve their own conditions. With the nation's economy guided by their leaders' actions under the review of the Treasury and Federal Reserve, they can be sure that future booms and busts will be avoided. The Federal Reserve and Treasury will manage the financing of the nation's expenses in a rational, commonsense manner. With the individual citizens given the freedom to make their own choices in a nation that grows into an industrial trading nation, opportunities for financial growth will surface. The individual citizens at local levels will improve their lives and finances. As individuals improve their conditions, the local governments will improve their operations and finances. With local governments improving their operations and finances, states will improve their economics as they all combine activities. With each state and local area improving its economy by using its local resources, the nation itself will improve its economy.

Freedom's nation will become a reality with a few important changes over the next several years. The changes that the nation will need are the following:

1. Identify political leaders who understand the principles that founded this great nation.
2. Elect leaders who believe in the freedom of the individual that God gave to all as a right.
3. Reorganize the federal government to give more power and authority to the states.
4. Audit the organization that manages the nation's finances: the Federal Reserve.
5. Correct the faults of the Federal Reserve that have caused this country's financial problems.

6. Reorganize the Federal Reserve and Treasury to manage the financing of the government.
7. Give value to the dollar using the market price of gold.
8. Review and limit the major entitlement programs.
9. Review, limit, and change the nation's military strategy.
10. Use the country's natural energy sources and nuclear technology for an industrial renaissance.
11. Build economic growth, jobs, and opportunities with individuals, local businesses, and regional state industries.
12. Revive the nation's business goal to one of international trade, as it was in the seventeenth and eighteenth centuries, to provide growth of economic opportunities and employment.

It is understood by the author that all of the above will take time, and that there is a major hurdle to overcome. The major hurdle is the unfounded belief that a state or government organization possesses intelligence and abilities that are superior to those whom it governs. The founders of the United States were intelligent and experienced in business and public service operations. They had experienced governance by a country that had strong, centrally controlled leadership. In order to avoid replacing the governing authority that they had experienced with a similar one, they created a government that gave strength and authority to those who were governed. This worked successfully for approximately 135 years, creating a strong industrial trading nation. The nation has gone from a powerful industrial nation to a weakened, consumer-dependent nation with record deficits that it struggles to reduce. It has a chance to make the above changes to bring itself back to being Freedom's Nation as it once was.

HOW DID THE UNITED STATES GET TO THIS POINT IN TIME?

In 1913, the Federal Reserve was created to become the nation's third central bank. The Federal Reserve and third central bank were meant to solve the problem of periodic national economic downturns that had resulted from poor financial management of the nation's banking and business industries. With the creation of the Federal Reserve, future banking and financial crises were supposed to be avoided, while funding of the nation's government expenses would be provided.

Though the creators of the Federal Reserve promised that future banking crises would not occur, less than seventeen years later, the country was in the Great Depression of the 1930s. This happened because the ease of funding banks and financial transactions allowed the "Roaring Twenties" to develop. The ease of funding the economy led to allowing financial organizations such as banks to give high levels of credit to businesses and individuals that became excessive in 1929. When loans for businesses, and stocks in those businesses, failed due to excessive speculation, a stock market crash happened in October 1929. In spite of the promises of the Federal Reserve that bank failures would be avoided, hundreds of failures occurred during the Depression years.

It was during the Great Depression that John Maynard Keynes wrote *The General Theory of Employment, Interest, and Money*. Because he advocated deficit spending during economic downturns, he was credited with helping the United States to come out of the Depression. In fact, many modern economists and historians believe that preparation for participating in World War II by the country's industries brought back hiring and increased industrial output. Booms and busts that followed from normal economic business activities have given Keynes's theory of deficit spending credit for the nation's economic improvements over the years.

The Federal Reserve has used Keynes's theory of easy money availability to stimulate the economy several times over the years. Although booms were often encouraged by lower-than-practical interest rates, when recessions happened afterward from people cutting back from overspending, increased money availability would end recessions. Until 1971, the Federal Reserve could implement deficit spending during recessions to increase consumer spending. Before then, the dollar and budgets had to limit expenses to keep from raising the number of dollars to equal an ounce of gold. With more dollars in circulation and no increase in the value of gold, inflation would show up in the price of goods and services. With too many dollars and no change in gold, inflation would indicate the need for the Federal Reserve to raise interest rates to stabilize the standard of living for citizens.

Once the Federal Reserve did not have a measure to a real, market-based substance such as gold, the Fed was able to use the Treasury to print dollars. With the Treasury printing dollars, the Federal Reserve could set interest rates to whatever level was needed to sell US bonds. With spending from 1968 federal programs that Lyndon Johnson and Congress passed, and new programs that Congress enacted in the 1970s budgets, inflation grew through the 1970s. In the 1980s, under a new chairman of the Federal Reserve named Paul Volcker, the Fed slowed inflation and brought stability to the economy. Raising interest rates and slowing the creation of dollars was not the normal operation of the Federal Reserve. Volcker's term as chairman of the Federal Reserve ended in 1987. From 1988 to the present, the Federal Reserve has provided as many dollars as needed at lower-than-normal interest rates to ensure that Congress will have however many dollars it needs to fund federal expenses.

When the Federal Reserve resumed providing low rates and abundant dollars during the late 1990s, the economy grew at a stable rate. From the mid-1990s until the next decade, the Federal Reserve provided below-normal interest rates to fund many congressional bills that supported a growth in the housing market. In spite of a boom in housing, the Federal Reserve provided low rates and increased funding for budgets with high military expenses. As was done in the 1970s, the Fed provided abundant funds and low rates that inflated the cost of living while satisfying the voting public.

In 2007 and into 2008, the Fed continued to feed a housing boom and growth in the economy. In 2008, the growth in housing, and the accompanying loan volumes, overloaded several large financial operations and caused them to go bankrupt. The bankruptcy of several financial firms, and the loss of business in the housing industry, caused a huge loss of jobs and loss of property values. With no limit to how much money the Fed and Treasury could create, many billions of dollars were spent to keep many banks and some large industrial companies (AIG, General Motors, and Chrysler) from failing.

Economic activity, as measured by federal statistics, fell to its lowest level in the spring of 2009. To this day, the Federal Reserve continues to fund deficit spending of the federal government, in the belief that consumer spending will return and bring employment back to less than 6 percent (by federal statistics).

A SOLUTION INVOLVING THE FEDERAL RESERVE AND CONGRESS

Except for a brief time in the 1980s, the Federal Reserve has existed to provide as much funding as needed to allow Congress to pass whatever bills it needs. Because the Federal Reserve Board is made up of the twelve regional banks of the country, it operates to satisfy those banks and the major customers of those banks. From this book's early discussions concerning central banks, the major criticism has been that the banks and their largest customers would get most of the attention, rather than citizen taxpayers.

The Federal Reserve knows that as long as it funds what Congress needs to buy votes in the next election, the majority of politicians in Congress will allow it to do what it wishes. What has developed is a unique relationship between the politicians in Congress, the Federal Reserve, and the Treasury. The Federal Reserve board and the Treasury Secretary do not question what the majority of Congress passes for legislation. Congress people who wish to stay in office support the Federal Reserve. Those members of Congress who believe in the state or federal government having authority over the individual get their bills funded by the Fed. Since the Federal Reserve does not have any allegiance to the individual citizen, it ensures that whatever bills Congress passes are funded.

Many members of Congress know little about economics, but they do know that providing benefits to citizens gets those votes. More citizens benefitting from a Congressional bill that passes gets Congress more votes. The unique relationship between Congress and the Federal Reserve needs two improvements:

1. The Federal Reserve board needs to be composed of leading members of the business community, rather than bankers who have not experienced the challenges of growing and operating a business.
2. The Federal Reserve board should not fund Congressional actions that do not, according to the business industry, follow logical business reasoning to determine reasonable costs.

With the Federal Reserve acting more as a conscience for Congress, it is possible that the politicians in Congress will better understand the values of their bills. Even the egos of politicians need a review of their work so that some benefits will reach the average citizen.

The thinking of members of Congress will have to change. The thinking of the last forty-five years has to change from thinking that deficits don't matter, and whatever Congress passes to obtain funding should get funded. With business leaders who have to justify their budgets and the results of their management on the Federal Reserve Board, Congress will have to justify its actions. Decisions on legislation will have to depend on long-term analysis of capital and operating expenses that make sense in terms of growth and improvement of the nation's operation.

Spending simply to gain votes will need to also consider that tax dollars from citizens' earnings will have to pay for those expenses. As any businessperson knows, spending to solve problems, without having income and revenue to pay those expenses, does not eliminate the problems. Spending to simply gain favor from a customer (voter), while not helping that customer to improve his or her income, will only cause the business to fail. If the customer has to spend more than he or she makes, it will not take long for the customer's operation or household to fail.

As previously mentioned, both the businessperson and the customer must decide what the return on their investment provides for them. With businesspeople acting as the conscience of Congress, it is more likely that Congress will give more thought to legislation than to how much campaign funding, organization dollars, and voters' support they can gain. It is unlikely that leading businesspeople will make unerring decisions, because history has shown that no business has worked without making mistakes. At one time—perhaps in the late 1800s and early 1900s—bank leaders actually managed their own money or the money of their largest depositors. Bank leaders of today manage the money of all depositors in their banks. Those depositors are citizens, businesses, and large organizations. Bankers manage other peoples' money and not their own.

The bottom line is that bank leaders are corporate politicians who gained their status by pleasing those at higher-level positions in the organization. The bank leaders who sit on the Federal Reserve Board got there either through politics in the banking community or through the educational or university community. Because much of the university education in economics and training to work in the Federal Reserve has centered on the Keynesian theory of deficit spending, commonsense business management has been ignored. The leaders of the US economy from the banking community do not understand business management.

What will it take to bring about changes in the way that Congress thinks?

1. Freeing the individual and moving the authority over operation and management of government from the central government to the states.
2. Keeping the Federal Reserve Board at twelve members, to represent each of the twelve regions of the United States.
3. Choosing board members via a governor's committee from each region, nominating a leading businessperson from his or her region. Those board members would represent the business community and citizens in each region.
4. Both the senators and representatives from each region must approve the nominated board member for their regions.
5. The Federal Reserve Board members would choose which board member would be the chairman.
6. Budgets from Congress must be reviewed and approved by the Federal Reserve Board before approval by both houses of Congress.

With free individual citizens, and the leadership of the country focused on trade with other countries, the strength of the states and their economies will build businesses in each US region. The governors of the states within each region will support the growth of businesses within their states and within their region. With the personal improvement that comes from free individuals, their businesses, and industries that enjoy their work, the general economics of city and state governments will progress. State governors will not only benefit from improving their states' economies but will also assure that their governments and the national government supports that progress.

Therefore, the choices for the board of the organization that guides the economy will be critically important to them. The status of each governor's state will depend on the economic performance of his or her state. The choice of Federal Reserve Board member for each region will determine the influence of the Federal Reserve Board on the governors' states and regions. Members of the two houses of Congress from each region will support the nominated board member because it will be important to them that their region does well economically. Once the Federal Reserve Board is set, then it can operate similarly as it has in the past. The Federal Reserve Board and Treasury will manage the operations of national banks. The Treasury will issue currency to meet the level of money needed to supply the bond levels approved by the Federal Reserve Board. The Federal Reserve Board will review the national budget and submit the level of budget expenses that it approves to provide a strong, stable, growing economy over the next twenty years. Congress must adjust its budget to ensure that the country will have a strong long-term future and growth to provide a steady and secure economy for its citizens.

The role of the Federal Reserve in review and funding of government expenditures will be different from what the country has experienced over the last forty-five years. The use of gold to support the value of the dollar will help ensure that inflation is controlled, while booms and busts are avoided. The value of a free-market commodity as the basis for the currency will give adequate readings of inflation of other commodities that make up the cost of living. The potential of over exuberance in the pricing of real estate, stock exchanges, and limited software markets will be avoided, as items will be compared to a stable free-market commodity such as gold. The interest rates on US bonds will be determined by a free international market rather than set by purchase of bonds with a currency that has no basis of value. With the national debt under control and the national deficit decreasing to a minimum, the demand for US bonds will be strong. With trade increasing with other nations and inflation under control, the title of world reserve currency will be preserved.

The Federal Reserve Board representing the business community in each region will have a gradual influence on the actions of Congress. Members of Congress will try to please the citizens in their congressional districts, and will be concerned with how their actions impact the business community. Rather than simply viewing the business community as potential donors, Congress will need to look at how their actions impact the citizens as customers of businesses. Business leaders from different regions will look at legislation by Congress and the president with a view toward how those actions will influence businesses similar to their own. Board members, instead of viewing legislation as simple expenditures, will look at those actions as affecting their own business or similar businesses. Legislation will no longer be viewed as dollars required for funding with other peoples' money, but will be looked at as something that could influence their own money.

With the Federal Reserve Board taking a personal interest in legislation, the members of Congress will have to justify their actions to people similar to citizens in their own districts. It will take time, but Congress will eventually have to change its attitude and actually serve the citizens in their home districts instead of deciding what benefit they can provide to buy some votes. This will bring about a change in congressional members and will change the way that Federal Reserve Board members work.

HOW WE WILL BENEFIT FROM A SOLUTION INVOLVING THE FEDERAL RESERVE AND CONGRESS

Citizen taxpayers will see Congress and the Federal Reserve working for the long-term good of the nation in providing opportunities for work and the ability to progress in their lives. Federal government programs will be focused upon providing opportunities for individuals to improve their lives. Those individuals will have a government that encourages businesses without restrictions on spending more time and money on preventing risk. Rather than government preventing risks to individuals, it will encourage individuals to seek more opportunities for themselves and the businesses for which they work.

Without the risks that the founders of this nation took with their lives, the country would not have become a strong industrial trading nation at the beginning of the nineteenth century. The promise of funding the national government to carry out its programs can be realized by funding it to give all citizens the opportunity to take chances to improve themselves and their country. It has taken over one hundred years for the United States to realize that individuals and their governments (local, state, and federal) must take risks to obtain rewards. As it was intended by the founders of the United States many years ago, the citizens of this country must be freed to pursue their destinies.

"We hold these truths to be self-evident, that all men are created equal, that they are endowed by their Creator with certain unalienable rights. That among these are Life, Liberty, and the pursuit of Happiness."

Above are but a few lines from the Declaration of Independence, which was delivered by the colonists to Great Britain. What followed was a revolution that created the United States of America. The Constitution and Bill of Rights that followed it guided the country to becoming strong enough to overcome the costs of lives and expenses of a Civil War and two world wars. As with the growth of people, it takes setbacks to teach lessons to help improve future performance. The Civil

War taught the country that all men were created by God as equal. The two World Wars, the Vietnam War, and the conflicts in the Middle East taught the world that aggressive military actions cost the aggressor more than they cost the victim. It is hoped that Congress, with review by a Federal Reserve more geared to the citizen population, will conduct itself to prevent harm unwarranted to others by aggressors.

What can evolve over the next few years is a revolution back to what started this nation. Individuals will be able to take risks to improve their lives by making their own free choices. Governments will guarantee their freedom instead of restricting it to manifest the strength and authority of a single central government. Governments will allow the common sense of individuals to make choices, to live their personal lives, to make positive improvements that benefit themselves—as long as they do no harm to others. Discriminatory decisions that do no physical or monetary harm to others will be judged by citizens in an atmosphere of freedom of choice and ability to make just decisions. The government programs that begin at the federal level will be established by a Congress and Federal Reserve Board that uses common-sense business rather than politics. The direction of government will be more agreeable to the general hardworking, responsible, independent citizens who seek to improve themselves and their families.

Members of Congress will eventually become the public servants that the first members of Congress actually were. The members of Congress who founded this country risked their lives and property to represent people in their home states. Being a congressional public servant in 2030 will involve a different level of thinking. These members will have to really identify with voters in their home areas. It will not be a game to see what benefits can be offered in a trade for votes. Politicians will truly need to be people who want to serve their citizens in a way that is best for them in the long term. Choices will have to be made by congressional politicians that may disagree with the media and with liberal arts educations that populate the media. Logic, common sense, and long-term thinking will have to overcome emotional, short-term, minimum-work, and high-benefit thinking. Some of the courage exhibited by the founders of this country will be needed to overcome the beliefs in entitlements that have developed over the last fifty years. Members of both political parties became believers in a strong central government to guide the poor, ignorant citizens. Both political parties believed in providing benefits to gain a bloc of votes. Whether the blocs of votes were from high-income executives or low-income entitlement recipients made little difference to the politicians. Only a very few members of Congress really acted as true public servants, doing and voting for what was best for all citizens. This became very apparent from the low opinions expressed by polls of citizens concerning Congress and the president.

With the revolutionary changes made throughout this book in place by 2030, the United States can have a true representative government. Representatives at the federal level of government will truly be working in the best interests of the citizens in their state and country. The country will be a stronger, more independent country that has reverted to functioning as the founders desired. The nation will live up to the words of Abraham Lincoln in 1863:

> **Four score and seven years ago our fathers brought forth on the continent, a new nation, conceived in Liberty, and dedicated to the proposition that all men are created equal.**
>
> **Now we are engaged in a great civil war, testing whether that nation, or any nation so conceived and so dedicated, can long endure. We are met on a great battle-field of that war. We have come to dedicate a portion of that field, as a final resting place for those who here gave their lives that that nation might live. It is altogether fitting and proper that we should do this.**
>
> **But in a larger sense, we cannot dedicate—we cannot consecrate—we cannot hallow—this ground. The brave men, living and dead, who struggled here, have consecrated it, far and above our poor power to add or detract. The world will little note, nor long remember what we say here, but it can never forget what they did here to the unfinished work which they who fought here have thus far**

so nobly advanced. It is rather for us to be here dedicated to the dead we take increased devotion to that cause for which they gave the last full measure of devotion—that here highly resolve that these dead shall have a new birth of freedom—and that government of the people, by the people, for the people, shall not perish from the earth.

What President Lincoln said and what followed from amendments to the constitution reinforced the intent of the Declaration of Independence. It set a standard of freedom that helped guide the nation to growth and improvement that helped it through two world wars and two depressions. With new leaders in Congress and the Federal Reserve, the nation can recover from the latest great recession and renew the promise that the nation's founders desired. The country will not only be stronger but will also lead in industry, trade, income, employment, freedom, and international relations. The United States will have positive relations with all of the most economically active nations, to ensure that trade with them and all key productive nations can benefit both parties. Though the politics and beliefs of other nations may differ from those of the United States, this country will be respected and understood by all. **The United States will have become the country that was once known as Freedom's Nation.**

www.ingramcontent.com/pod-product-compliance
Lightning Source LLC
Chambersburg PA
CBHW060045210326
41520CB00009B/1275